So We Live, Forever Bidding Farewell

Theology & Assisted Dying

— JOHN PARRATT —

Sacristy
Press

Sacristy Press
PO Box 612, Durham, DH1 9HT

www.sacristy.co.uk

First published in 2020 by Sacristy Press, Durham

Sacristy Limited, registered in England & Wales, number 7565667

British Library Cataloguing-in-Publication Data
A catalogue record for the book is available from the British Library

ISBN 978-1-78959-109-5

Who has turned us around, so that
whatever we do we are in the posture
of someone who is departing? As if he,
on the last hill that shows him all his valley
again for the last time, turns, pauses, and lingers—
so we live, forever bidding farewell.

Rainer Maria Rilke, *Duino Elegies*, Eighth Elegy

Contents

Foreword

Forty years ago, as a neighbouring parish priest, I was invited to become chaplain to one of the first hospices, at Mount Vernon in Middlesex. The fact that it was a National Health Service and not a religious foundation made it for me all the more interesting.

At the time I knew nothing about palliative care, and saw my role through a pastoral lens, being there, as best as I could, to love, to listen, and to be alongside the terminally ill and their families. The subject of this book, "assisted dying", was never mentioned. It was simply assumed that those who were terminally ill would be cared for to the end of their lives and their pain eased as far as possible, but with no thought of an early end.

This book is a brilliant, compassionate and skilful examination of what must now be one of the most compelling questions of our time: How can it be right to withhold release from those who are terminally ill, who are in extreme pain, and for whom life has no longer any dignity, purpose or meaning? Archbishop Desmond Tutu put it like this:

> I wish to help to give people dignity in dying. Just as I have argued firmly for compassion and fairness in life, I believe terminally ill people should be treated with the same compassion and fairness when it comes to their deaths. Dying people should have the right to choose how and when they leave Mother Earth. I believe that alongside the wonderful palliative care that exists, their choices should include a dignified assisted death.[1]

His words come at a time when members of the medical profession are rethinking how best they can support the terminally ill, when increasingly there are debates on the subject in Parliament, and when all the signs show a shift in public opinion. There are no easy answers. But for me this book sets out clearly and brilliantly the way in which perhaps we should be beginning to think. It would be an invaluable tool for any who have the privilege to be alongside those whose lives are coming to an end.

The Rt Revd John Richardson
Bishop of Bedford (1994–2002)

Acknowledgements

I am most grateful to Sacristy Press for undertaking this project, and especially to the Commissioning Editor, Dr Natalie Watson, for her helpfulness and meticulous attention to detail.

In the writing of this book I have been greatly helped by the comments and advice of several relatives and friends. My thanks are due especially to my daughter, Dr Rachel Parratt, both for advice on the medical material and reviewing the whole manuscript; also to my brother, Professor Jim Parratt, and to Dr Irengbam Mohendro Singh for additional comments on the medical data; to Gillian Massiah and the Revd Geoffrey Ravalde for advice on legal questions; to Val Tyler for commenting from a personal and pastoral perspective; and to Dr Tom Anderson for supplying materials which would otherwise not have been available to me. Of course, the views expressed in the book are my own and should not be attributed to those who have kindly reviewed the manuscript.

I owe a very special debt to Bishop John Richardson for reviewing the argument from his extensive experience in end of life ministry and for consenting to write the Foreword.

My thanks are also due to Aristeidis Pathanaglou for advice on the translation of the poem from modern Greek by Gryphius, and to John Finney for permission to use his photograph of Borrowdale, which so beautifully illustrates the extract from Rilke's *Duino Elegies* from which I have taken the title of this book.

John Parratt
Carlisle, June 2020

Abbreviations

AV	Authorised (King James) Version of the Bible (1611)
JPS	*Tanakh: a new translation of the Holy Scriptures according to the Hebrew Text* (Jewish Publication Society, New York & Jerusalem 1985)
LXX	The Septuagint (Greek translation of the Old Testament)
RSV	Revised Standard Version of the Bible (Nelson, Edinburgh, London & New York 1952)
BMA	British Medical Association
BMJ	British Medical Journal
CPS	Crown Prosecution Service
DPP	Director of Public Prosecutions
NHS	National Health Service
NICE	National Institute for Clinical Excellence
ONS	Office for National Statistics
PHE	Public Health England
RCP	Royal College of Physicians

In the midst of life we are in death[2]

Death and dying: a changed situation

The great Austrian composer Joseph Haydn, towards the end of his life, remarked to his biographer Griesinger: "I am no more use to the world. I have to be waited on and tended like a child, it is high time God called me to himself." Haydn died at the age of seventy-seven in May 1809, after a long career in which he became known as "the father of the symphony and the string quartet". His final years were spent in increasing ill health and mental fatigue. Six years earlier he had sent to his publisher, unfinished, his last major work, a string quartet of which only the two middle movements were completed. His frailty convinced him he would be unable to complete it. There was no decline in his religious faith—this was the man who routinely began his scores with "in the name of the Lord" and ended them with "thanks be to God", and who apologized for making his music "too cheerful", because "at the thought of God my heart leaps for joy". Inspiration had not quite deserted him, but the mental and physical strength to bring that inspiration to fruition had left him. The end of life seemed emptied of meaning.

I suppose that many of us who have been privileged to live to a "ripe old age" have had similar feelings. What we could do in earlier youth and in the maturity of middle age deserts us. The decline may not be into senility or complete physical collapse, though this is sadly too often becoming the case in our modern world. But there is the realization that we have reached the "[L]ast scene of all that ends this strange eventful history".[3] I am reminded of my academic doctoral supervisor, who at the age of 102 is reported to have remarked, "I feel I should no longer be here"; or of a voice from the pews saying, "I am less worried about dying than about living too long!" It is not perhaps surprising that the words of Keats' *Ode to a Nightingale*, written when, at a young age, he was dying of a then incurable illness, resonate with an increasing number of people:

> . . . for many a time
> I have been half in love with easeful death,[4]
> Called him soft names in many a mused rhyme
> To take into the air my quiet breath.
> Now more than ever seems it rich to die,
> To cease upon the midnight with no pain.

What has been euphemistically termed "the dying process" has come to the fore in the twenty-first century in a way not experienced by earlier generations. It has been estimated that at the time of Jesus the average lifespan was just twenty-eight years. Up until 1800 it was still only around forty years, and even in 1900 it had reached only fifty-two for women and forty-nine for men. A century later, at the turn of the millennium, due to improved living standards and the astounding advances in modern medicine and technology, life expectancy had increased to eighty-one for women and seventy-six for men.[5] Politicians and social commentators describe this increase in life expectancy as "a good thing". But a Public Health England (PHE) report suggests that for many it can sometimes be far from a good thing. On the plus side, their data indicate that the average person can expect sixty-three years of tolerably good health. On the other hand, we can also expect between sixteen and nineteen years of ill health—up to a quarter of a lifetime. Socio-economic inequalities have a stark effect both on longevity and quality of life. For the poorest in society, PHE reports life expectancy may be up to nine and a half years less than for the wealthier, and they could face up to nineteen more years of ill health than the richest. Predictably the age profile of the population of the UK has changed dramatically. In 2018, there were an estimated 1.6 million persons over eighty-five, three times more than in 1971, and the prediction is that by 2031 there will be over two million in this age bracket. The economic consequences of this are immense. Whereas previous generations, with far fewer elderly to cope with, tended to absorb care for the elderly within the family (often burdening daughters, and in

Asia daughters-in-law, and effectively denying them a fulfilled life), the nuclear structure of the modern family and the increase in the number of single people makes this increasingly problematic. The so-called crisis in the NHS is caused less by lack of the will to fund it adequately than by the huge demographic age shift. Providing quality healthcare for the increasing numbers of elderly people is a financial dilemma which seems to have little chance of being solved.

In one sense, the spectacular advance in modern medicine has been a victim of its own success. There is now almost an expectation that medical treatment can cure virtually everything, and there is increasing pressure on doctors to prevent death at any cost and to go to great lengths to bring about the impossible end of restoring even the very elderly to youthful vigour. The realization that "the ageing process", as it is quaintly called, is simply the body wearing out, often causing multiple conditions and illnesses, may be tacitly acknowledged. But the fact that there is "a time to die" (Ecclesiastes 3:2) is all too often pushed under the carpet. Bishop Richard Holloway has complained that death and dying have been taken over by the medical profession. It has, he says, "wheeled in formidable artillery onto the battlefield and spent vast sums of money and effort in delaying death's victory . . . with the best of intentions (doctors) have taken control of the lives of old people today, and they fight hard to keep them in the field as long as possible".[6] If that sounds unduly harsh, here is an eminent surgeon making a similar point, and commenting on the failure to see the patient as a *human* being rather than a medical problem to be solved:

> Scientific advances have turned the process of ageing and dying into medical experiences, matters to be managed by the health professionals. And we in the medical world have proved alarmingly unprepared for it . . . This experiment of making mortality a medical experience is just decades old. It is young. And the evidence is that it is failing.[7]

Gawande goes on to say that as medical advances have taken the extension of the lifespan far beyond what would have been thought possible a few decades ago, we are in danger of forgetting what it is to be mortal. Mortality, he asserts, has become "a medical experience to be managed by professionals". Here he is also highlighting a related problem, the outsourcing of dying and death from the family to the less intimate care of hospitals, hospices and funeral directors.[8] If medical intervention has become too intrusive, it is as much because patients demand it as because medics do not wish to give up on their patients. We seem to have lost track of the reality that life is a finite commodity and that death is the inevitable final act before we shuffle off the stage. The psalmist reckoned that seventy years was about right (and that must have been an optimistic ripe old age three thousand years ago), and he realized life too had its problems.[9] However, recently a more realistic assessment of our limited lifespan seems to be making some impact. There is evidence that more patients are opting to reject invasive medical treatment and are choosing to die at home. Making serious preparations for death, planning one's own funeral, and drawing up "living wills" seem to be on the increase.

The website dignityindying.org.uk claims that 82 per cent of the UK population supports making assisted dying legal, and this includes some 78 per cent of "religious" people, and that nearly half of that number would be willing to risk prosecution (currently fourteen years in prison) by assisting a loved one with terminal illness to die. It further claims that 54 per cent of GPs are either neutral or supportive of assisted dying. These results may be questionable and the methodology in reaching them is unexplained. Nevertheless, even if these claims are themselves only 50 per cent accurate, it indicates that there is a large moiety of the population, including convinced Christians, who would support making assisted dying available. Church leaders as well as elected MPs are evidently out of touch with their publics.

Death and dying: a Christian theological approach

What has come to be known as "assisted dying"[10] has been approached from the perspective of several different disciplines—medical, sociological, ethical, and so on—and has spawned a considerable literature both in print and on the internet. Much of this literature treats the issue on the basis of agnostic or atheist assumptions, and some would argue that these are the only valid bases on which to participate in the debate on assisted dying, and that to introduce religion into the argument is a distracting irrelevance. From a Christian point of view, this stance is quite wrong. To the contrary, I want to argue that the debate about assisted dying actually goes to the heart of what Christian belief is all about, and that basic theological categories should provide the ground and basis for discussion within the Church and society at large. Questions such as: What is the nature of the human person? What do "life", "death", and the possibility of life after death mean? What is the meaning of pain and compassion? These questions go to the heart of the Christian faith. But not only the Christian faith: whether we like it or not, much of our Western ethics is built on the Judaeo-Christian tradition, and therefore it can still usefully inform us on hard ethical questions. For me this tradition has to be rooted in the Bible as the foundation source document of the Christian faith. But even the best of our English translations are inherently unable to convey the full implications of the original languages. I have therefore in places had recourse to the Hebrew and Greek terminology to try to bring out the deeper meanings of the text itself. But biblical and theological concerns will also need to be brought into debate with medical and sociological arguments about assisted dying. So while this book is primarily addressed to clergy, the churches and individual believers, hopefully it may also be useful to readers who approach the issue from a non-religious perspective.

Official church statements have uniformly condemned assisted dying, but ironically have based their position more on non-religious than on theological arguments. A striking example of this was the debate at the General Synod of the Anglican Church in 2012 on the Falconer proposals on assisted dying. Despite these being rejected *nem con*, subsequent developments suggest that the Synod was by no means as unanimous as it appeared, and that potentially dissenting voices were not adequately listened to. But there have also been prominent Christian leaders who have spoken out clearly in favour of assisted dying. Surprisingly it was a Roman Catholic theologian, Hans Küng, who first publicly brought assisted dying (called then "voluntary euthanasia") to general attention in a seminar primarily addressed to the German churches.[11] Küng regarded the issue as "too important to be left to the decisions of (medical and legal) specialists", and argued that "our own dying can be discussed afresh in a sober, dignified and morally serious way, and without dogmatism and fundamentalist reasoning". Subsequently Paul Badham published his pioneering *Is there a Christian Case for Assisted Dying?* which directly challenged the prevailing opposition to assisted dying among Anglicans.[12] He pointed out that "the authority of Christianity is normally claimed by opponents of euthanasia, though they rarely appeal to Christian premises in the debate". Ironically Badham's book was criticized by an evangelical reviewer (unfairly, I believe) for not being biblical enough. However, the generally positive reception of his book indicated that he had eloquently argued a case of which many were increasingly becoming convinced. Assisted dying was then supported by two former Anglican archbishops, George Carey,[13] who reversed his previous opposition to it, and Desmond Tutu in South Africa.[14] But by and large the attitude to assisted dying on the part of the churches has been a forthright rejection, the Catholic and more conservative wings being most opposed.[15] While this position has been claimed to be based on biblical Christian principles, it seems to me that it has too often lacked theological depth and been based on questionable biblical exegesis—or even lacking in biblical references.[16] This is regrettable since, as suggested above, assisted dying involves fundamental theological questions. But it is not just a matter of dispassionate theological reflection, rather for many people today assisted dying is a very urgent and personal dilemma. It is a new problem which historical theology has not generally found it necessary to come to grips with.

My aim in this book, then, is to try to set assisted dying in the wider context of Christian faith, of how Christians understand the nature of human existence, life and death, and the ultimate destiny of human beings. Only on this basis can we ask whether assisted dying can be regarded as a legitimate option for a Christian believer. If it can be an option, then the second question is: "under what circumstances?" In trying to answer this, the question of the nature of pain (in the psychological as well as the physical sense) and when it can be regarded as unbearable, will have to be addressed. And since the individual act of assisted dying necessarily involves another person, and of course the wider community of family and friends, the question of compassion, and how we should understand it, arises. In attempting to make sense of assisted dying from a theological point of view, we shall need also to remind ourselves that we are dealing with an intensely personal problem, which cannot be adequately assessed simply by academic, medical and philosophical, or even detached theological, arguments. It is (to use a much-overused word) an existential issue which goes to the heart of what we are as human beings. For many it will be something which may not be considered seriously until they are brought up against it in a very personal way. It is for this reason that I have included, especially in chapters 1, 3 and 5, historical and contemporary examples of those who have themselves faced this dilemma. The Christian virtues of compassion and empathy will be as important as the more doctrinal understanding of what it means to be a human being subject to mortality.

However, I am seeking here to address assisted dying primarily within the context of those who are dying of terminal illness and who are mentally capable of exercising their own decision-making autonomy. Quite different questions are raised regarding assisted dying for those who have lost the mental capacity to make rational decisions for themselves, or for those who have not yet reached maturity, and for whom the future discovery of a cure may still be possible. These are, of course, also debates which ought to concern the Church and wider society, but they are not part of the main discussion of this book.

1

Death will be welcome to close my eyes for ever[17]

Is there a Christian understanding of death?

There is probably no more profound treatment of death and dying in literature than in Shakespeare's *Hamlet*, as much for its deep psychological insights as for the beauty of its poetry. Even before the curtain rises, we have a case of fratricide, and by the time the play ends, the stage is literally littered with corpses—death by poisoning in several different ways, drowning, accidental and deliberate homicide. And besides all this we have the profound soliloquies of Hamlet debating with himself the pros and cons of suicide. All that is lacking is a character who dies peacefully of old age in his own bed. Clearly there are many and varied ways of dying. The layperson's perception of death from pre-modern times was the cessation of breath, often interpreted as the departure of the spirit or soul from its prison house of the body—though this reflects a Greek philosophical understanding rather than a biblical one. Modern medicine identifies two stages in the dying process. Clinical death is the heart ceasing to beat: resuscitation is possible at this stage. Biological death, usually occurring about five minutes or so later, is the failure of the brain cells from lack of oxygen. Those who oppose assisted dying tend to make a sharp distinction between a "natural death" from old age or illness,[18] and an unnatural one, which would include, alongside death by violence, suicide and assisted dying. But it seems to me that dying is more complex than that rigid dichotomy would allow. In this chapter, I want to try to analyse different ways of dying, and the often misleading terminology we use for these, and to suggest that we should understand these different ways of dying more as part of a continuum.

For the ancient Hebrews death was the "common lot of all mankind . . . to die as all people do" (Numbers 16:29; also Psalms 78:39 and 90:3, 9–10; Isaiah 40:6–7). The earliest Christians clearly understood death as quite normal. The narratives of raising the dead in the Gospels were not intended to be normative, and the resurrection of Christ was interpreted as an altogether unique act of God.[19] Paul (despite the apparent belief in an imminent "second coming" of Christ) continues to use the pre-Christian euphemism of the dead as having "fallen asleep".[20] Augustine, however, found in Paul's writings a connection between physical death and sin, leading him to formulate the doctrine of original sin.[21] The traditional foundation of this doctrine is found in the myth of the "Fall" in Genesis 3.[22] In the narrative, disobedience results in death. Presumably the author of Genesis understood the threat "in the day that you eat of it [the tree of the knowledge of good and evil] you shall die" (Genesis 2:17) not as indicating that physical death would be the instantaneous result of disobedience. Rather it means that mortality would enter into human life (judging by the longevity of the ancestors in Genesis 5, physical death remained a very distant prospect!).[23] The Old Testament nowhere interprets this passage to make a direct connection between Adam's sin and death, still less that it infected all future humanity. The doctrine of "original sin" is not part of Jewish belief, and thus cannot be attributed either to the earliest Jewish Christians or to Jesus himself. Paul, to be sure, does seem to make a connection between the sin of Adam and physical death in Romans 5:12–17 and 1 Corinthians 15:21–2.[24] Probably Paul accepted the literal meaning of Genesis 1–3. But his interpretation of this passage is a *midrash*[25] (as in 1 Corinthians 10:4; Galatians 4:22–6). His argument is that there is a contrast between Adam as representative of human sin and mortality and Christ as the bringer of righteousness and life. The literalist understanding of this passage can have a potentially damaging effect on the experience of dying, since it teaches that death is a consequence of each person's sin (through Adam) rather than simply a natural human process.[26] All this is not, of course, to say that Christian theology fails to take sin seriously as a rupture in relationship with God, or disregards the need for forgiveness and reconciliation. Jesus himself insisted that wickedness lies within the human heart (Mark 7:15).[27]

The biblical language of sin and righteousness probably finds much less resonance in a modern culture which has less familiarity with the Bible. It is not surprising then that modern theologians have sought to express its relevance in a different terminology. Existentialism in particular has brought the shadows of human life into the light.[28] This is especially so with regard to death and mortality. John Macquarrie reminds us that "it is death, more than anything else, (which) brings before us the radical finitude of our existence".[29] He makes use of the category of disorder to interpret the biblical doctrine of sin. Disorder encompasses the experience of alienation, from ourselves, from others, and from God. It is a sense of incompleteness, a failure to live up to our own ideals, and also of lost-ness and ambiguity. The fact of our human mortality, the inevitability of our own death, makes us aware that the life we experience is both transient and contradictory (well expressed in Psalm 39:4–6). This sense of finitude, and the futility of our temporal concerns, is reflected in Jesus saying, "What does it profit a man, to gain the whole world and forfeit his life?"[30] For the existentialist theologian Paul Tillich death threatens our being with "non-being", nothingness.[31] For an atheist existentialist (like Sartre) this leads to a sense of the profound meaninglessness of life. For the Christian it leads to an acceptance of death with the confidence that it cannot destroy the conviction that we are accepted by God in an indestructible relationship. Thus either death is the ultimate absurdity of annihilation which renders life meaningless, or it points to something greater beyond ourselves, namely God.[32]

Historical understandings of death

In his seminal book *Western Attitudes toward Death from the Middle Ages to the Present*[33] the French historian Philippe Ariès identifies four major periods in history which in his view illustrate quite distinct attitudes towards death. In the earlier period, he argued, death was simply accepted as a fact, and the rituals surrounding death were open and public. He termed this "tamed death", since death was seen as normal and neither feared nor avoided. During the medieval period, Ariès believed, death came to be regarded as more personal, largely due to the impact of the Church's preoccupation with divine judgement after death. This was the period of "one's own death". The early eighteenth century saw an abrupt change in attitude. Death was no longer seen as normal, but rather as something to be feared. It was alien, a disruption to normal human life. This change of perception, Ariès argues, led to an increase in mourning rituals and the desire to preserve the memory of the departed—the period of "Thy Death". Ariès' fourth period begins around the turn of the nineteenth to the twentieth century, which he calls "a brutal revolution" to the era of "Forbidden Death". Death became a taboo, a subject to be avoided, and the process of dying shifted from the patient's bedroom, surrounded by his or her family, to the hospital. Death was no longer under the control of the dying and their family, but was in the hands of doctors, and increasingly funeral professionals.

Ariès' reconstruction is stimulating, but almost certainly flawed. His sharp periodization makes no allowance for the fact that attitudes towards death must have been, in all periods, far more varied and complex than his schematization suggests; nor does it admit of the large cultural variations within Western societies.[34] His material is based rather less on empirical data than on depictions of death in art and literature, which do not always reflect the public perception. Further, the Catholic eschatology of judgement, with its threats of purgatory and hell, was challenged in the sixteenth century by the Reformation doctrine of salvation by faith, which in some cases led to a more positive embracing of death. Large exceptions can be found in all of Ariès' periods in attitudes to death.[35] As Kenneth Boyd has pointed out in his perceptive paper on historical attitudes to death,[36] Ariès' "tamed death" was not at all tame, since many people did not die in their beds but in war, epidemics and famine.[37] Perhaps more important (as we noted in the introduction) death was "normal" not only because of low life expectancy but also because of high infant mortality rates—even in eighteenth-century Europe child deaths before the first birthday were (according to the Office of National Statistics) as high as 15 per cent. And it is perhaps instructive to remember that Jesus himself lived in a world in which life expectancy would have been between thirty and forty years. Consequently, what we regard as an adult life began at a much earlier age. Marriage for men was common at around eighteen, for women even younger. By this time a man would already be practising his profession or working with his hands. It is likely then that the disciples would have been, by our standards, very young men at the time of their calling. Jesus' death at around thirty or so, though violent in the extreme, would not have been unusually young. We have to beware of imposing our models of youth, maturity and age on a very different time and place. Reading the Gospels in the light of this can radically modify the way we understand both Jesus' actions and his teaching.

The calamitous events at the beginning of the twentieth century, World War I, in which there were around ten million military and seven million civilian deaths, and the ensuing worldwide influenza epidemic of 1918 (with fourteen million deaths in the former British Empire alone) simply do not fit Ariès' theory. The first, with the establishment of war graves and war memorials, marked a further shift, that of the public memorialization of death. But if Ariès' periodization of attitudes to death is exaggerated, he is right to draw attention to the modern practice of outsourcing death and burial to hospitals, hospices and the funeral industry. Gawande points out that "swift catastrophic illness is (now) the exception", and that "for most death comes only after long medical struggle with an ultimately unstoppable condition".[38] In recounting the parting of one particularly seriously damaged patient, he confesses that he really could not understand what dying actually means. "Medical science", he writes, "has rendered obsolete centuries of experience, tradition, and language about our mortality and created a new difficulty for mankind: how to die".[39]

Traditionally death meant cessation of breath, a view reflected both in the Hebrew scriptures (the giving up of the *nephesh* or *ruach*). The late biblical Book of Ecclesiastes speaks of "the dust [i.e. body] returns to the earth as it was, and the breath [spirit] returns to God who made it" (Ecclesiastes 12:7). But this reflects a Platonic view rather than an Israelite one. For Plato the soul was immortal, the material body perishable and subject to moral as well as physical corruption. When cessation of brain activity is added to cessation of breath, it seems to give credence to Gawande's conundrum that death includes the process of dying as well as the actual point of departure. It is easy also to see how the medicalization of dying has obscured the fact that, from a theological point of view, dying (especially in older age) is normal not abnormal. The contemporary African theologian Kwesi Dickson has pointed out that in African tradition "the death of an old person is accepted as a natural consequence of age".[40] He quotes a Yoruba prayer: "that we may not die young, that we may not attain an age of wretchedness." This is much closer to the biblical understanding than the desire to prolong life at any cost. This perception of "a good death" as a fitting end to life, death as a fulfilment rather than as an enemy to be resisted at all costs, is surely one that needs to be recovered. In the words of Ecclesiastes: "for everything there is a season, and a time for every matter under heaven: a time to be born, and a time to die" (Ecclesiastes 3:1). But can there be a time to take death into one's own hands?

Taking one's own life

Consider the case of Chretian Urhan. He is known to Christians today (if at all) as the composer of the tune (Rutherford) subsequently set to the hymn "The sands of time are sinking".[41] But Urhan was much more than a minor composer. He was in fact one of the most accomplished musicians of the early nineteenth century. A virtuoso on the violin, viola and viola d'amore, he became the principal violist of the Paris Opera orchestra. Nicknamed the "Paganini of the viola", he became so famous that several composers included solo and *obligato* parts for the viola and viola d'amore for him in their works.[42] Urhan was a devoted, almost mystical Catholic, and in later life became organist of one of Paris' prominent churches. His faith was austere and self-denying in the extreme, and he lived frugally and gave most of his money to charity. When he was first appointed to the opera orchestra, he accepted the post only on the condition that he could sit with his back to the stage so that he would not be distracted by the charms of the female singers and dancers. In middle age, Urhan suffered a stroke during a performance. He subsequently decided to end his life by starving himself. He suffered terribly in the process and died, surrounded by friends, in 1845. The Catholic Church, whether aware or not of what was technically suicide, nevertheless celebrated his funeral in the Cathedral of Notre Dame. We may surmise that, when it was no longer possible for Urhan, because of physical disability, to practise his life's passion for music, he chose to embrace willingly his more overriding passion, communion with God.

Urhan was not the only prominent Christian to have had a favourable attitude towards suicide. Over two hundred years earlier the metaphysical poet John Donne had penned what was probably the earliest defence of suicide by a Christian in the Western world. After a somewhat unsettled early life, Donne took holy orders on the advice of James I in 1615, and later became Dean of St Paul's Cathedral. In 1608, he had written *Biathanatos, declaring the Reasons, the Purpose, and End of the author*.[43] In the Preface, Donne recognizes that his work will offend many, but he argues, referring to John 5, just as there was no healing until the waters were troubled so "the best way to find truth in this matter was to debate and vex it". He alludes to Beza's attempt to commit suicide by drowning himself and confesses, "I have often had such a sickly inclination."[44] *Biathanatos*[45] has been understood by some critics autobiographically—it is claimed it was written at a time when Donne's life was in disarray and he was suffering acute melancholy, and himself contemplating suicide.[46] This seems to me unlikely since the argumentation is coherent and surprisingly objective, even detached. It seems rather that Donne is exploring a genuine dilemma (a "paradox" characteristic of the metaphysical poets). His aim is to present a thesis and open up a discussion—a brave thing to do considering attitudes to suicide at the time. *Biathanatos*, he says, "is a declaration of the paradox, or thesis, that self-homicide (as Donne terms it) is not so naturally a sin that it may never be otherwise". His argument is that taking one's own life depends on the circumstances in which it is done and is an individual decision. Giving up one's life is exercising a choice which we have been given, to exert our control over our own death.[47] Suicide, then, is not a sin in itself, it all depends on the context in which life is given up. Thus in the Old Testament Samson and Saul were justified in their actions because of the exigencies of war. Donne does, however, have a caveat: suicide can become sinful when it is the result of despair, pride, self-interest, fear of suffering, or a desire for the afterlife. These are fairly daunting restrictions, and Donne admits that since suicide is *likely* to be done for these reasons it is appropriate that it should remain illegal. Clearly, limiting suicide to an act carried out for a good reason is moving the discussion to a consideration of what today would be called martyrdom, voluntarily suffering death for commitment to an exceptional cause. Donne's focus here (as in much of his religious writing) is on the example of Christ, which, he argues, shows that giving up one's life voluntarily and willingly is justified when it is done out of charity, that is, for the good of others. Jesus, he argues, not only willingly submitted himself to death, but also "gave up his spirit".[48] This was "self-homicide", an example to us that we should lay down our lives for others.

Donne, as we would expect, knew his Gospels. It is clear from the Gospel narratives that Jesus regularly risked a violent death—as C. H. Dodd once put it, he willingly put his head into the lion's mouth. His ministry shows that he provoked antagonism by actions and words which under the Law were punishable by death (Mark 2:7; 11:18; 14:63).[49] His determination to go to Jerusalem, a pivotal moment in the Gospel narrative (Luke 9:51), presaged a violent end like that of some of the prophets (Luke 13:33–4). The three-fold prediction of the Passion (Mark 8:31; 9:31; 10:33) is often taken by biblical commentators to be a *vaticinium ex eventu*. But while these texts may have been elaborated later by the evangelists, it is likely that, as Joachim Jeremias argued, these sayings go back to an original Aramaic *mashal*.[50] The eucharistic words point in the same direction, and it is clear enough that Isaiah 53 underlies both Jesus' own and the early Christian understanding of his mission. The Fourth Gospel reflects the same tradition in the discourse of the Good Shepherd who lays down his life for his sheep (John 10:11, 14, 17). We shall return to the implications of the death of Christ in relation to the legitimacy in surrendering one's life below, though of course for Christian theology the crucifixion of Christ is of far greater significance than simply as an example of a martyr's death.

However, strong condemnation of suicide prevailed in the West, largely on religious grounds. In this it drew upon Jewish tradition rather than that of Plato (who argued that people could commit suicide if they were no longer able to contribute to the state). The rabbis based their rejection of suicide on the basis that the time of a person's death is in the hands of God alone (Ecclesiastes 3:2), and that it is a sin to anticipate this appointed time. Interestingly they did not base this opinion on Exodus

20:13 but on Genesis 9:5. After Constantine, the Church intensified its antagonism towards suicide, and it became a crime. Since successful suicides could hardly be punished extreme measures were put in place to discourage it. Even in nineteenth-century England the estates of suicides were forfeited to the state and their bodies could not be interred in sacred burial grounds. In Louis XIV's France the bodies of suicides were mutilated and desecrated and left on garbage heaps. Suicide was only officially decriminalized in Britain in 1961, the same year in which assisting suicide became a criminal offence. In fact, suicide accounts for very few deaths in the UK, and regrettably it is more likely to be committed by younger people than the very elderly. In 1981 (when figures began to be collected), suicide accounted for just 14.7 deaths in 100,000. In 2017, there were 5,821 persons over ten years of age who took their own lives (which was the lowest recorded number in all years since 1981).[51] But according to the ONS, instances of suicide rose in 2018, mainly due to a worrying increase among young adults.

It may be helpful at this point to consider the origins of the terms "suicide" and "martyrdom" and the motives for them. The actual term "suicide" is quite a late invention and is not known before around 1650. It was coined as a euphemism for "self-killing" or "self-homicide",[52] but soon came to attract the same stigma and opprobrium (we might compare a similar process in the replacing of "assisted suicide" by "assisted dying"). Probably the earliest systematic treatment of the subject was the French sociologist Emile Durkheim's *La Suicide*.[53] In pursuance of his general approach, Durkheim tried to understand suicide almost exclusively from the standpoint of the relationship of the individual to society as a whole.[54] His two classifications of suicide which are most relevant to this study are egotistical suicide and altruistic suicide. The former is caused by the conviction that the person does not really belong to his or her society. Lack of integration leads to "excessive individuation", and isolation from one's fellow citizens, which in turn leads to despair. The second, altruistic suicide, results from the sense of not being valued by society—hence he argued that in a truly altruistic and caring society there should be no suicides. But this type of society may cause, or even at times require, the individual to sacrifice his or her own life to preserve the ethos of the society. The most obvious case of this is to give one's life in defending society from aggression, especially in warfare. It could also perhaps include those who lay down their lives defending individuals or a group of companions, or for a deeply held cause which benefits society as a whole. An example of this would be the suicide of Lawrence Titus Oates on Scott's ill-fated expedition to the South Pole in 1912. On the return journey, suffering from severe frostbite which slowed down his companions, Oates chose to leave the tent and walk to his death in a blizzard. The threat of committing altruistic suicide has also sometimes been used to exert moral influence on oppressors. The most well-known case is perhaps Gandhi's threats of "fasting to the death" in protest against British colonial policies and the violent riots which accompanied Indian independence.[55]

Martyrdom is akin to suicide in that it involves surrendering one's life, but is distinguished from it in that it involves others taking that life, usually violently. The word derives from the Greek *martus*, literally a witness, and is used frequently in the New Testament in that original sense (e.g. Matthew 18:16; Acts 1:8,22). In the context of religious witness, *martus* comes to have the meaning of one who witnesses by his or her own death. This meaning also has its roots in Jewish history, especially in the turbulent years of the second and first centuries BC. There are references to giving up one's life to uphold faith in God in the Apocrypha and Pseudepigrapha which come from this period. The Jewish historian Josephus gives two graphic examples, one of mass suicide and the other demonstrating the readiness to die for religion.[56] It is possible that early Christians regarded Jesus as their first martyr—Revelation 1:5 calls Jesus "the faithful witness [*martus*], the firstborn of the dead". The Church early on accepted the view that death was preferable to denying one's faith. The Book of Acts records the martyrdom of Stephen (7:60) and James the brother of John (12:2)—the second almost in passing as though death for the faith was not unusual. Acts subsequently has a detailed account of Paul's journey to Rome, where he was later beheaded. Elsewhere in the New Testament, there are references to the precarious situation of confessing faith in Christ (e.g. 2 Timothy 4:6; Hebrews 12:4; 1 Peter 5:10; 1 John 3:16; Revelation 2:13; and probably 1 Corinthians 13:3). At the end of the first century, the letters of Ignatius suggest that for some Christians martyrdom was actually welcomed.[57] After Constantine, martyrdom became less of an issue for Christians, though at times the Church indulged in its own persecutions of pagans and Jews, who were also martyred for their religious beliefs. But reverence for martyrs soon became a cult within the Church and a new "army of martyrs" was produced by persecution of those regarded as heretics and in the conflicts of the Reformation.[58]

Suicide and martyrdom both involve the willing offering of the individual life. Martyrdom differs from suicide in that it involves others who actually take the life of the martyr, usually out of violence towards the victim or the faith which he or she holds. But the fact that someone else does the actual killing does absolve you from the moral responsibility of putting yourself into the path of death. Refusal to save your life by recanting carries the same responsibility for your own death as does suicide.[59] One of the most moving examples of this is the case of Edith Stein. She was born into a large observant German Jewish family and became a nurse during World War I. Stein subsequently received her doctorate in philosophy from the University of Göttingen, and taught at the University of Freiburg, where she was influenced by Heidegger's existentialism. She converted to Roman Catholicism and joined the Carmelite order as a nun. Falling foul of the Nazi Nuremberg edicts against the Jews, she and her sister Rosa (also by now a nun) were sent by her order to Holland. She wrote a moving letter to Pope Pius XII (which remained unanswered) beseeching him as the "Father of Christianity" to condemn Nazi oppression and persecution of Jews. Even at this stage she was contemplating willingly offering up her life as a "sacrifice of atonement for peace". When the Nazis overran Holland and she was destined to be sent to Auschwitz, she refused an offer to escape the country, being "determined to share the fate of her brothers and sisters". Along with Rosa she perished in the gas chambers in 1942. She was canonized as a martyr by Pope John Paul II in 1998.

Suicide and martyrdom, then, both involve the personal decision and responsibility of accepting death as the right option. But what if another person administers the cause of death on behalf of the person who has made the choice? In the winter of 1935, Viscount Dawson, George V's doctor, is said to have remarked to Prime Minister Baldwin that the king was "packing up his luggage and getting ready to depart". The king had been ill for some time. A heavy smoker, he had to have oxygen available in his bedroom.[60] By the January of the following year, while the king was staying at Sandringham, it became clear that he was dying, and his condition was exacerbated by an attack of bronchitis. He was deeply concerned over the affair of Prince Edward with Wallis Simpson, and had already finalized his will and the matter of the succession with his advisors. His physician at the time, Bernard Edward Dawson, had graduated from London University, had an MD, and was President of the Royal College of Physicians. Dawson had a distinguished war record and a string of honours, including a viscountship. On 20 January, he issued his bulletin that "the King's life is drawing to a close". The expectation was that George would die that night, and Dawson had already telephoned his wife to instruct the editor of *The Times* to hold his publication, so that the king's death could be reported on the front page of the morning edition—it was strongly felt that the event should be released by *The Times* as the most respected newspaper and not by the lesser regarded press. The king, however, lingered on, and Dawson was concerned that prolongation of his life would seriously affect the arrangements that had been made. Alone with the king except for a nurse, he decided to administer an injection of morphine and cocaine, and George died at five minutes before midnight.[61]

Such an act of administering lethal drugs to a patient is euthanasia. But here (as with suicide) the original meaning of the word has become debased. Euthanasia means "a good death",[62] and is used in that sense in classical Greek. The term bore the meaning of "an easy death" in English up until the seventeenth century. The pejorative use of the word became common only two centuries later. Wyatt is probably right to draw attention to the little-known essay by Samuel Williams published in 1870, which advocated the use of chloroform to end cases of hopeless and painful illness, but only when this was desired by the patient's express wish.[63] But he is quite wrong (especially in the context of his complaints about "the use of ambiguous and misleading terminology by campaigners") to go on to condemn euthanasia on the basis of historical misuse of the term. Perverted evolutionary eugenic theories and practices have no place in a rational discussion of euthanasia nor any relevance to it, nor do the atrocities of the Holocaust. It should hardly be necessary to point out that these things were the result of a failure to recognize our common humanity and treated people as things to be manipulated. They did not result from any consideration for the patient, which is the point of euthanasia in its proper sense.

The Oxford Dictionary, more realistically, defines euthanasia as intentionally ending life by the "painless killing of a patient suffering from an incurable disease or irreversible coma". The NHS similarly defines euthanasia as "the act of deliberately ending a person's life to relieve suffering". Both these definitions emphasize that the motive for the act does not stem from evil intent but from compassion. Medics have refined this understanding to distinguish between active and passive euthanasia. While the former involves some positive action on the part of the doctor (or another person) by, for example, administering drugs or lethal injection, the latter (sometimes called "pulling the plug") involves stopping treatment in one way or another. The latter is legal in some countries. But somewhat controversially the NHS distinguishes passive euthanasia explicitly from the act of withdrawing life-sustaining treatment "in the patient's best interests". It maintains that the latter act (withdrawing life-sustaining treatment) "can be part of good palliative care and not euthanasia". It is difficult for the layperson to appreciate any material significance in this nice distinction. It raises several crucial issues: How is commission (giving drugs to hasten death) different from omission (not giving necessary treatment or deliberately stopping it) when the result will be the same?[64] From the point of view of consequentialist ethics this distinction cannot be upheld. Nor can it from a moral standpoint, for in both cases the ultimate *intention* is to end life. Intention is central to the teaching of Jesus (especially in the Sermon on the Mount), so the distinction is also theologically invalid. It seems to be a convenient medical distinction, the purpose of which is to make one way of ending life more acceptable than another, but which does not have a sustainable ethical justification. And from the patient's point of view would not the withdrawal of treatment usually cause more pain and distress to the patient? Above all *who* is it that determines what is "the patient's best interest"? We shall have to return to these questions subsequently.

Related to euthanasia, but much more drastic, is the concept of mercy killing. Perhaps the best-known example of this in recent times is associated with the conflict with Japan in Burma (Myanmar) in World War II. The Chindit campaign, masterminded by Orde Wingate, involved guerrilla warfare behind the Japanese lines to disrupt their attacks on Imphal and Kohima.[65] It was one of the most vicious and dangerous campaigns of the war. Mortally wounded soldiers who could not be evacuated were given morphine or even shot to avoid their falling into the hands of the Japanese invaders. One is reminded of the case of Saul (1 Samuel 31:1–5). Wingate, the maverick commander of the Chindits who determined their tactics, was in fact a devout Bible-believing Christian and a member of the conservative and fundamentalist Plymouth Brethren. Presumably he did not regard mercy-killing as inimical to his faith in God.

Because of the frequent pejorative or misleading use of the term euthanasia, the increasingly preferred terminology today is "assisted dying".[66] The NHS defines assisted dying as "the act of deliberately assisting or encouraging another person to kill themselves". Aside from its defective grammar, this attempt at a definition raises several serious problems. Most problematic is that it puts the onus on the assister, whereas the word "assisted" clearly should mean that he or she is only helping, providing assistance to a patient who has already made the decision to end his or her own life. Further, and perhaps more important, the insertion of the phrase "encouraging another person to die" is quite gratuitous. There may well be people who press others to end their lives (not least on so-called social media), but this has nothing whatsoever to do with assisted dying. "Assist" means precisely that—to help to facilitate the enactment of a decision which the individual has made prior to the actual dying. In those countries where assisted dying is legal the patient has to affirm this is indeed his or her wish. Assisted dying involves not merely the compliance of the patient but an active desire to die as quickly and painlessly as possible. The Cambridge Dictionary definition is much closer to the reality: assisted dying is "the act of helping someone who wants to die to kill themselves when they are too ill to do it alone". Similarly, the neurosurgeon Henry March affirms: "Assisted dying is not euthanasia. It is about people who make their own choice that it's time for their life to end." In the nature of the case, accurate statistics on the number of those who take their lives by assisted dying in the UK are uncollectable as it is a criminal offence. One estimate in 2014 put numbers at around three hundred over the year: subsequent reports claim that there has been an increase of around 75 per cent in those seeking assisted dying in Switzerland, and that (according to Dignity in Dying) there is one such case every eight days. Whatever the facts, it seems clear enough that the option of travelling outside the UK to avail oneself of assisted dying, despite the fact that the assister may still be liable to prosecution, is being taken up by an increasing number of terminally ill patients.

From this brief survey of the terms and methods of taking one's life a number of facts emerge which may inform the assisted dying debate. One is that neutral terminology which originally bore no ethical implications (suicide, euthanasia) is now being employed by some writers in a deeply pejorative sense, and it would appear the use of "assisted dying" by its opponents is moving in the same direction. This trend is not helpful to an objective debate. Secondly, it is probably better to understand these terms more as points on a continuum of taking one's life, than of sharply opposed options. Finally, Donne's thesis makes a very valid point: each case is an individual one and generalization (especially if it is condemnatory) is misleading. For Donne, the individual circumstances and the motives for desiring death are all-important. We shall return to these points subsequently.

2

What a piece of work is man[67]

What does it mean to be human?

The previous chapter focussed on mortality, the ways in which life can end. But what is the nature of the human person who dies, what does it mean to be a human being? This question is answered differently by different disciplines—biology, sociology, philosophy, and so on—which have their different methodologies and presuppositions. Here I am concerned only with the theological understanding of humanity (so-called theological anthropology), which for the Christian will underpin all other approaches. I am in agreement with Rowan Williams that "when it comes to personal reality the language of theology is possibly the *only* way to speak well of our sense of who we are and what our humanity is like—to speak well of ourselves as expecting relationship, as expecting difference, as expecting death".[68] In other words, a purely secular understanding of human nature is inadequate, because it leaves out of the account our relationship to God, who is the ground of all existence and being. The "Christian doctrine of humanity" has occupied volumes, but I am here only interested in those aspects of it which seem to me of direct relevance to the assisted dying debate. Perhaps the most important is the paradox (neatly set out in Hamlet's speech) that mortal human beings, "this quintessence of dust", are endowed with gifts which point to a higher nature than simply physical life.

The biblical view of the human being is dynamic rather than static; "human" is not an abstract construct, but a living acting reality. Its writers are not interested in philosophical universals, but in the real existence of human beings. In fact, the biblical languages have no words which correspond exactly to an ontological concept of "human nature".[69] The

Genesis creation myth expresses human beings' god-like qualities under the symbol of human beings as being created in the "image and likeness of God" (Genesis 1:26–7; 5:1). This symbol is not found elsewhere in the Old Testament, nor is it defined in detail. It is probably to be understood against the background of the strict obligation not to represent God in any material form, encapsulated in the first of the Ten Commandments (Exodus 20:4–5) and repeated again and again in the Hebrew scriptures. The nature and being of God is not reflected in material and inanimate objects made by human beings, but is reflected only in living human beings, in their personhood, self-awareness, and moral nature. It is not surprising that Paul sees the image of God as supremely manifested in Christ (2 Corinthians 4:4; Philippians 2:7; Colossians 1:15) and in the renewed nature of believers (Ephesians 4:24).

The psalmist gives us a similar view. He sets humankind within the context of the splendour of God's creation, and marvels at the power and authority with which God has endowed him:

> What is man that you are mindful of him,
>   mortal man that you have taken note of him?
> That you have made him little less than divine,[70]
>   and adorned him with glory and majesty.
>
> *Psalm 8:4–5 (JPS)*

But at the same time as celebrating humankind's "glory and majesty" the psalmist uses words that also point to human frailty and vulnerability,[71] and to our mortality. The sequel to the creation myth, the story of the Fall of humanity, puts it in similar terms: "you are dust and to the dust you shall return" (Genesis 3:19).

How may we interpret the biblical picture of humanity in modern terminology? Macquarrie uses the term "transcendence" to describe human beings.[72] Transcendence is the recognition of something greater and beyond ourselves, but in which we also share. What characterizes human existence, in Macquarrie's view, is self-awareness, that a human being—in contrast to the rest of creation—is "open to his being, in the sense that he not only *is* but is aware that he is". This self-hood is always developing, "is always on the way, always incomplete at any given moment".[73] Human beings are the only creatures who possess the dynamism and vitality actively to change their environment by the exercise of both reason and will. Transcendence, then, includes the idea of growth; human existence is not static but always (hopefully) moving forward. This sense of incompleteness involves the possibility of choice, whether for good or ill, to which we shall return below.

Being human involves *relationship*, above all relationship with God. But this relationship inevitably involves also a relationship to other created beings. Thus Paul Tillich, in his classic *The Courage to Be*, argues that the first meaning of existential is "the attitude of participating with one's own existence in some other existences".[74] Rowan Williams has explored relationship to God as the foundation of life in his lecture "What is a Person?"[75] What makes me a person, he argues, "is the enormous fact that I exist here rather than elsewhere, being in relationship with those around me". So, he goes on, the person is "the point at which relationships intersect". The foundation of this relationship to others is, in his view, the fact of our relationship with God "by whom I have already been addressed, (for) in the Christian tradition before anything else happens I am in relation to a non-worldly, non-historical everlasting attention and love, which is God". Similarly John Webster, in combating the post-modern agenda which aims at dissolving human personality entirely, argues that "to be human is on the Christian account, to have one's being outside of oneself, to owe one's being to the being and activity of the triune God".[76] It is this which will determine our attitude to, and should seriously limit the exercise of, our freedom towards other human beings.[77]

This theme of relationship to God and to others is perhaps the main emphasis in Jesus' teaching. As Jeremias has it, "more important than anything else is the new relationship to God".[78] God is "Father",[79] the most intimate relationship possible. Though this form of address to God is rare in Palestinian Judaism, Jesus commonly employed it in prayer (Matthew 11:25; Luke 10:21; 11:2; 22:42; 23:34, 46).[80] It very soon passed into Christian liturgy and prayer (Matthew 6:9; Romans 8:15; Galatians 4:6). In the Pauline references the Aramaic familiar form *abba* is used, probably echoing Jesus' prayer in Gethsemane (Mark 14:36). However, for Jesus the father-son metaphor also reflects the flawed nature of human existence (Matthew 7:11). Thus a keynote in Jesus' teaching is the need for

repentance towards God, that is a challenge to "turn"[81] to the Father-God
and receive forgiveness (Mark 1:15; Matthew 6:4–15; Luke 15:11–32), and
to be "perfect" as God is perfect (Matthew 5:48).

The concept of life

Fundamental to what it means to be a human being is the concept of
life. It is unfortunate that the English word is somewhat inexact. Biblical
languages have a rich vocabulary associated with the idea of life. In
Genesis 2:7, we read that "God . . . breathed into [man's] nostrils the
breath of life,[82] and . . . man became a living being". The word here is
nephesh, that is a "living, breathing being". But *nephesh* also carries the
implications of mortality, the *nephesh* is given up in death. It does not
mean "soul" in the usually accepted sense. The New Testament uses a
number of words commonly translated in our English Bibles as "life".[83] The
usual word is *psyche* (which in AV is misleadingly translated as "soul"). In
the sayings in Mark 8:35–7 and Luke 12:20, Jesus is not talking about an
eternal soul but about the here and now earthly life being at risk (see also
Matthew 6:25; Luke 12:22).[84] Paul also uses "life" in this sense (Romans
16:4, also 1 Corinthians 15:45), where the contrast is between Adam as
a "living *psyche*" and Jesus as the "life-giving spirit" (*pneuma*). But the
New Testament writers also frequently employ another word for life, *zoë*.
This term indicates an altogether higher quality of life than *psyche*, usually
the messianic "life of the age to come", a life which cannot be affected by
physical death. *Zoë* is often qualified by the adjective *aiōnion* (translated
somewhat inadequately in our English Bibles as "eternal, everlasting").
We shall return to this in chapter 7. For the moment, we shall ask what the
characteristics of this physical life of ours are, and how they can inform
the debate on assisted dying.

   One theological tradition argues strongly that life should be
understood as a "gift" or "loan" from God. Nigel Biggar, whose position
is based primarily on the Aquinas tradition, makes a great deal of this
position. He argues that since life is a gift or loan we have no right to
destroy it.[85] While it may be agreed that for Christian theology God
is the source of all life, and not just human life, the idea that each

individual life is a special gift (still less a loan) does not seem to me to be prominent in the Bible. Advocates of the "gift theory" of individual life often also appeal to the concept of the "sanctity of life". Again, if what is meant by this is that every life is valuable in the sight of God, it is a valid point. However, those who base their argument on the "sanctity of human life" often go beyond this, and assert what could better be called "the inviolability of life", that is, that taking life in any way whatever is interdicted. The phrase "the sanctity of life" has a complex history. It seems to have occurred in discourse about taking life only in the 1970s, and then primarily in the context of abortion.[86] The Catholic theologian Heike Baranzke has made an important investigation into the origins and the meanings assigned to the idea of the "sanctity of life". She argues that the way the phrase is used in current ethical discussion is based on a fundamental misunderstanding. Its origin, she shows, lies in the frequent injunction in the Hebrew Bible, "Be holy for I (God) am holy", found primarily in Leviticus (11:44; 19:2; 20:7,26), and repeated elsewhere in the Old Testament. It is quoted as a Christian precept in 1 Peter 1:15–16. The Hebrew root *qdsh*, like the Greek *hagios*, is rendered in English by both "holy" and (as a verb) "to sanctify".[87] The term "holy" is used in an ontological sense of God alone. When applied to human beings, it never bears an ontological sense, as though human life was by nature holy or sanctified, but only a performative sense; it is an ethical demand to act in such a way as to approximate to the nature of God.[88] In biblical and Christian thought, God alone is ontologically holy, that is, has holiness as his essential being. When applied to human beings "holiness" or sanctity is not an ontological given, but a demand to *act* ethically. It is clear from this that the contemporary use of "the sanctification of life" in the sense of the inviolability of life has nothing whatever to do with its biblical origins. In fact, the Old Testament itself prescribes the taking of life for a number of crimes. It is of course legitimate to argue for the sanctity of life, in the sense of inviolability, on secular ethical grounds, though this would logically lead to a pacifist position, which has been only a marginal option for both Judaism and Christianity. Pacifism had normally been understood as non-violence towards *others* rather than to oneself. The concept of "the sanctity of life" then is not particularly helpful in the debate on assisted dying. It might be better if it were replaced by "the

dignity of life", or "respect for life", which seem to me to have a much
firmer theological justification. Though not in themselves biblical terms,
they have a solid grounding in the Prophets and Gospels. Unlike the
concept of the sanctity of life, respect or dignity do not immediately
shut down discussion on the validity of assisted dying. They leave open
to argument the question of what course of action best preserves human
respect and dignity.

A related, though less common, argument against assisted dying is
based on the concept of the "right to life". However, the *UN Universal
Declaration of Human Rights*, on which this approach is presumably
based, concerns those things which preserve and enhance the right to
live a full life—security of the person, protection against slavery, cruel and
degrading treatment, and other abuses. To use the argument of "the right
to life" against assisted dying is, as with the sanctity of life, an illegitimate
extension of this Declaration's basic intention.

Much more relevant is the concept of "the quality of life". The World
Health Organization's definition of Quality of Life is "an individual's
understanding of their [sic] position in life in the context of the culture
and value systems in which they live, and in relation to their goals,
expectations, and concerns". It goes on: "It is a broad ranging concept
affected in a complex way by the person's physical health, psychological
state, personal beliefs, social relationships, and their inner relationship to
salient features of their environment."[89] This statement includes mental
and psychological health as well as physical, and we might add to that
spiritual (in the widest sense) health as well. One might well express
. this in terms of "human wholeness", a concept which is very close to the
Hebrew *shalom*, usually translated as "peace" but which also includes
within it bodily and psychological wellbeing.[90] Quality of life, then, is a
subjective assessment by the individual, and not by any external agency
such as doctors or the law courts. It is certainly not the equivalent of
longevity. This is quite crucial as people in the developed world are living
longer, and often in the process acquiring life-limiting, chronic and
debilitating illnesses. Often those who suffer in this way may still have
what to them is an acceptable quality of life; it may be diminished but not
obliterated. Gawande gives several examples (including his own father) of
those overtaken by illness but who accommodated it and still preserved

for a time a tolerable quality of life. However, for some the process of living with a chronic debilitating condition may be an accumulation of losses as abilities are progressively stripped away, and there may come a point at which the individual feels that his or her very personhood is being lost.[91] In such a condition the question may become unavoidable whether any meaningful "quality of life" remains, or whether "life" has become a living death which may be brought to an end. This is a question which only the sufferer can answer, and involves the issue of *choice*, of human freedom.

Autonomy and assisted dying

How far we have the freedom to exercise choice, to, as it were, determine our own destiny, is controversial and raises the issue of human autonomy. While Martin Luther spoke of the "bondage of the will", Kant argued that we must be free if we are to obey moral commands. It is obvious that autonomy is never absolute, for we are all of us subject to the limitations imposed on us by our birth, and social, legal and political situations. In other words, personal autonomy is always constrained to one degree or another by the fact that we are also dependent. Rowan Williams, in his discussion of the problem of dependence, argues that, for the Christian, dependence is basically a question of being dependent on God, which he sees not as a legal matter but a moral one—dependence on God is a matter of trust or relationship. Our dependence is thus a condition of life which is rooted in the freedom which belongs to God in the exercising of his own liberty.[92] The search for personal identity therefore finds its origin not in the individual but in the freedom of God who has brought that person into being, and the freedom to act which God bestows on the individual.

Other theologians have also tried to grapple with this issue of what our freedom to act consists of. Karl Barth's christological approach seems to attribute autonomy to grace mediated through Jesus Christ. But this seems unnecessarily restrictive. It seems to me more reasonable to assume that it is part of human nature which is embedded in the creation narrative. "[O]f the tree of the knowledge of good and evil you shall not eat" (Genesis 2:17) implies that to be human is to have freedom to choose, especially to exercise moral choice. The whole tenor of the Old Testament agrees with this, most notably in the Decalogue. What is commanded must also be possible. The Emmanuel oracle makes it clear that there is a time in the life of the individual when moral responsibility kicks in, when knowing how to choose between good and evil takes place (Isaiah 9:15–16).[93] This is not, of course, to deny that there are deep flaws in human nature, sometimes termed heteronomy. But the whole thrust of the Bible is that choice is open to us. Jesus' teaching is summed up in these terms (Mark 1:15) as focussed on a call to repentance, literally to "change one's mindset", and many of the parables challenge us with a moral choice which (if they are to have any meaning at all) implies a certain freedom to choose. It is also significant that Jesus, in several of the healing narratives, explicitly asks the sufferer whether he wants to be healed (Mark 10:51; Luke 18:41; John 5:6); he does not override individual autonomy even in the interests of restoring wholeness to physical life. Some theologians, like Tillich,[94] locate autonomy in human rationality, but it is surely more than that. It is rooted in the will as well as reason and is a function of the whole person.

For the Christian autonomy is active participation in what is perceived and accepted as God's will. Autonomy must be seen as positive, not as freedom *from* external constraints but as freedom to act *for* good. In the New Testament personal freedom is often seen in this way (John 8:36; Galatians 5:1). But it is obvious that personal autonomy has to be exercised responsibly in relation to the needs of others, as we shall see in chapter 6. With specific reference to assisted dying, autonomy is not the basic question: the real issue is whether "active dying" can ever legitimately be perceived as God's will. One might respond that since belief in God requires us to be active in all our living, it is not unreasonable to believe that we may also, as circumstances dictate, be active, rather than simply passive, in dying. And there have been those, the Christian martyrs, who have acted in exactly that way (as we have noted in the previous chapter). Only humans, among all created beings, have the ability to end their own lives. "The gruesome capacity for suicide", wrote Franz Rosenzweig, "distinguishes man from all beings both known and unknown to us".[95] It is then part of a God-given autonomy, which like all other choices open to us may be used for good or ill.

Is there, then, for the individual person a right to die? As we noted above, autonomy implies a freedom of choice, but within certain constraints. Does Christian faith limit, or indeed forbid, the taking of one's own life under any circumstances whatsoever? The Church's traditional answer has been that it is inadmissible on the grounds of the sixth Commandment. However, it is clear that "Thou shalt not kill" is not meant as a blanket veto on taking life, whether your own or someone else's. Quite apart from killing in warfare (of which there is quite a lot in the Old Testament), the Mosaic code prescribed capital punishment for a range of offences, some of which seem to us in the twenty-first century relatively trivial (e.g. Leviticus 20:27; Deuteronomy 21:18; Numbers 15:33–6—the last for collecting firewood on the Sabbath). We cannot therefore simply assume that suicide, much less assisted dying, falls under the ban of Exodus 20:13. The assumption that taking one's life is contrary to the Bible and Christian belief persists, perhaps most strongly among Roman Catholics and more conservative Protestant Christians. An example of the latter is John Wyatt's *Right to Die?*, which has been widely commended by conservative evangelicals. Wyatt is an Emeritus Professor of Neonatal Paediatrics. While it is informative to have a contribution to the debate from such a viewpoint, it is not surprising that his book does not show particular biblical or theological rigour. Wyatt recognizes that patients have, under NHS guidelines, the legal right to refuse treatment and to withdraw themselves from life-prolonging treatment, which would have the effect of hastening death. However, for him this legal right does not justify a moral right to die. In his view, "those who wish to promote autonomy as the supreme good (which I am not sure anyone does, except perhaps manic dictators) should oppose the squandering of this ultimate value (i.e. autonomy) in self-destruction".[96] He regards autonomy as based on a false Enlightenment individualism—"I am the centre of my own universe", as he puts it—and considers that it is a modern invention that "we should have the right to be freed from the limitations of the created order". In his view, "true freedom is to live your life along the grain of the deep hidden order of creation".[97] It is not entirely clear what this last statement means in practical terms. If it means to live my life according to what I believe to be the will of God for me and for others, then it begs the question of whether dying can ever be the right option for me to take. Indeed, it seems to imply a "continue life at any cost" approach, which is an ideological position, not a theologically grounded one. Wyatt's stance here is based on a flawed superficial understanding of autonomy. As we have seen, in both religious and secular understanding, autonomy definitely does not mean I am free of all constraints to do whatever I wish to in order to benefit myself above others. There may well be cases in which "the right to die" may be exercised not primarily for *my* benefit (to relieve my pain) but for the benefit of loved ones who also suffer with me, of carers whose "right to live" may be put on hold and seriously disrupted in order to look after me, or on the wider scale (if we must deal in hard economics) because the costs involved in keeping me alive in old age could be more fruitfully spent treating younger people with their lives before them.

Of course, survivors will (usually) be deeply saddened by the dying (whether assisted or not) of a loved one. But the idea that a terminally ill patient should prolong his or her life, because to choose to die would be to exercise a wholly selfish act of personal autonomy, seems quite illogical. This is to allow a dogma to override the personal and *human*. The issue for the Christian is rather, "Does my personal autonomy as a human being created by God, with all the constraints that implies, include the choice in specific circumstances to take my own life, and if so, what would those circumstances be?" One of those circumstances is when the pain of terminal illness becomes so intolerable that to live has lost all meaning. We turn to this in the following chapter.

3

To cease upon the midnight with no pain[98]

What is pain?

In his autobiography, *On the Move: A Life*, the eminent neurologist Oliver Sacks gives a striking description of unpredictable paroxysms of sciatic leg pain which afflicted him, late in life, after a knee operation.[99] It had, he writes, "a quality of agony, of anguish, of horror . . . (in) intensity it was off the scale". Even an experienced and eloquent author like Sacks found it difficult to describe the pain in words: neuralgic pain of this level "crushes one into a quivering, almost mindless sort of pulp; all one's powers of will, one's very identity, disappear under the assault of such pain". It became so overwhelming that he was no longer able to read, think or write, and for the first time in his life he found himself contemplating suicide. Even the "huge doses of morphine" were largely ineffective to give him any relief. We normally think of pain (as one definition has it) as entirely physical, an unpleasant sensation deriving from damage to organs or tissues, caused by temporary or chronic illness or injury.[100] But medical science now recognizes that pain is much more complex than that. Gawande points out that it is not only the sensory nerves which are involved but also what he calls the "emotional and other output from the brain".[101] Professor Irene Tracey's research has used magnetic resonance imaging (MRI) scan images to investigate how different types of pain affect brain activity. Pain obviously has a positive function as an "alarm mechanism" to alert the sufferer to illness or injury. But mostly pain is unwelcome. Especially for the elderly, pains may be multiple, an unhappy reminder that as we age we may be subject to several different kinds of ailment.

This chapter is not intended as a clinical survey of pain, which is far beyond my competence. Rather I wish to isolate two aspects of pain which seem to me of relevance to the issue of assisted dying. Firstly, it is clear that pain is to some extent determined by social and cultural factors. Joanna Bourke argues that the pain event "is shaped by social and environmental interactions and by their historical context".[102] The idea of what constitutes bearable pain differs from one cultural context to another, and also changes throughout history. New means of ameliorating what in earlier generations would have been unavoidable pain has changed our conception of what level of pain is regarded as bearable. Furthermore, it has been amply demonstrated that pain tolerance is higher in some professions than in others, and that in some cases painful injuries become almost normalized. Athletes and especially ballet dancers frequently have a very high pain tolerance threshold, which is no doubt due in part to the perception that success in their particular activities may necessarily involve enduring physical pain. It has also been asserted that genetic factors may be important. According to Erin Young of the University of Connecticut, mutations of the SCN9A gene may be a factor in determining the body's response to pain.[103] In some very rare cases individuals have been found to have no sense of pain whatever, a condition which is not entirely beneficial as it seriously handicaps medical diagnosis.[104] Individual levels of pain tolerance may therefore differ widely. This is of relevance in that it makes it extremely difficult, if not impossible, for doctors both to determine the degree of pain their patients are experiencing and the level of medication which is appropriate.[105] This will be especially problematic in the case of the terminally ill. While it is no doubt true that many people die without experiencing significant pain, the level of opioids such as morphine to be administered to lessen the pain of death can hardly be an exact science.[106]

Secondly, and perhaps as a corollary to the previous point, pain is an essentially *personal* experience. No one, however empathetic or medically aware, can truly feel the pain of another. Sacks' description of his own pain as "from the inside" indicates how hard it is to express pain in all its physical and mental aspects in words. Bourke suggests that pain is "outside language" and "absolutely private and untransmissible"—it is notoriously difficult to explain in words exactly what it feels like, which makes it a serious problem for communication between patient and physician! This might be why verbs used in both biblical languages to give voice to pain are drawn from the inarticulate cry of animals.[107] But there is also a paradox here: while pain is essentially personal and individual, it does somehow have to be communicated to others if relief or comfort is to be sought. And this communication is not simply with the doctor, but also with those who will respond in the compassion which is as important as the medication. We shall return to a consideration of this in the following chapter.

Pain: a theological exploration

While we are primarily concerned here with end-of-life pain, it will be useful at this point to explore briefly the theological approach to pain in general, and more relevantly, whether faith in God does, or may, ameliorate individual pain.

The biblical understanding of pain is complex. The writers of the Hebrew Bible were well aware of the symptoms of sickness (see for example the detailed descriptions in Leviticus 14 and 15). They also, incidentally, refer to pre-modern forms of treatment (e.g. 2 Kings 20:9; Isaiah 1:6; Jeremiah 30:12–13). But bodily pain does not seem to be their primary concern. Rather there is more interest in pain as a psychological and emotional experience and in a deeply traumatic fear of its future calamitous consequences (e.g. Isaiah 13:8 and 26:17; Micah 4:10). It is notable that the imagery for pain which is drawn upon here is not taken from severe illness or physical wounds but the pain of childbirth.[108] In the Psalms, pain is less physical than emotional, symbolized by the hatred from enemies who are often (as in Psalm 22) pictured as wild ravenous beasts. Perhaps the most extreme expressions of such psychological pain are found in the Book of Jeremiah. We might today characterize Jeremiah as something of a manic depressive. His prophecies contain a series of interpolated complaints (sometimes called the confessions of Jeremiah),[109] which reveal the intense internal struggle of his relationship with God—at one point he even accuses God of enticing him (20:7). Why, he asks, is his pain so endless and his wound incurable (15:18)? No less than three times he regrets and curses that he was ever born—a kind of proleptic suicide wish (15:10; 20:14,18). Jeremiah certainly suffered physically in his lifetime, but the pain here is entirely mental, a darkness which cannot be overcome and which issues in a death wish. By contrast the unnamed prophet of the exile whose oracles are recorded in the second part of the Book of Isaiah, uses the powerful imagery of physical illness in the last of the so-called Servant Songs (Isaiah 52:13–53:12).[110] The Servant is portrayed as a leper, "the many were appalled at him—so marred was his appearance, unlike that of a man, his form beyond human semblance" (52:14). He is "a man of suffering, familiar with disease", and like the leper he "hid his face from us" (53:3, JPS).[111] The description of the Servant as "smitten and afflicted"[112] also reflects the imagery of debilitating sickness. The suffering and ultimate violent death of the innocent Servant (vv. 7–8), however, become a metaphor for expiation of sin and transgression (v. 5). The pre-Hellenistic church saw this passage as prefiguring the passion and death of Christ (Acts 8:26ff.; Romans 15:21; 1 Peter 2:24–5), though Matthew 8:17, more literally and following the Hebrew rather than the LXX text, applies it to the healing acts of Jesus.

The association of the physical sickness of the individual with sin is fairly often met with in the Old Testament. It was perhaps a mistaken conclusion drawn from the philosophy of history we find in the Deuteronomic corpus.[113] The question put to Jesus in the narrative of the healing of a blind man (John 9:1–2) shows that the assumption that sickness was punishment for a former sin was still current in his day, and he strongly refutes it. It was this idea which the poetic drama of the Book of Job sought to counter. Job gets no explanation for why God allows suffering. His search for explanation comes to an end only in the light of the overwhelming theophany of the last chapters. God, as Abraham Heschel remarks, is the reasoning beyond absurdity.

The Gospels have little interest in describing the pain of illness or of death. While there are many accounts of individual healing, and many more comments on mass healing,[114] few mention symptoms. The fullest descriptions of physical symptoms concern cases of psychiatric illness, attributed in the first century to demon possession (Mark 5:1ff. cf. Luke 8:26ff.; Mark 9:14 cf. Luke 9:37ff.). The two occasions in the Synoptic Gospels of resuscitation give no detail on the pain associated with death.[115] More remarkably, though crucifixion was probably the cruellest and most agonizingly prolonged death ever devised, there is no detailed description of the physical pains of Jesus' death (apart perhaps from the reference to thirst, John 19:28). The most powerfully moving incident in the crucifixion narrative reflects mental torment rather than physical, in the cry of dereliction, "My God, my God, why have you forsaken me?"[116] The mental agony reflects a sense of abandonment, a sense of a broken relationship.

In parts of the Old Testament, the pain of broken relationship is metaphorically applied to God himself. In his seminal but undeservedly neglected book, the Japanese theologian Kazoh Kitamori was probably the first writer in modern times to explore the relationship of God and Christ as one involving divine pain. His *Theology of the Pain of God* was published in 1947 in the aftermath of Hiroshima and the occupation of Japan by the allies.[117] Although the book is primarily an exploration of the "pain of God" in the event of the crucifixion of Christ, Kitamori has taken his title from a phrase in Jeremiah 31:20, which he translates as "my heart is pained for him".[118] In a passage set within the context of the misery of Israel in exile and the promise of restoration, God affirms "therefore my heart is pained for him" and that he will have mercy. For Kitamori pain is part of God's essential being, and he reinterprets the patristic concept of "being" (*ousia*) accordingly. He argues that the patristic theology of the impassibility of God is mistaken,[119] and that for God to embrace us requires a God who has pain. While his book is primarily about the relationship of pain between God and Christ, he also claims that it is "God in pain who resolves our pain". [120] The pain of God is communicated in a special way by the suffering of the man Jesus, and thus "gives meaning to our pain".[121] Conversely, we know the pain of God through our own pain, which becomes the "symbol" of the pain of God, and it is in this sense that he interprets those passages in which Paul speaks of "suffering with Christ". His point is that human pain is not an end in itself, but rather should lead to practical action in the service of the pain of God.[122] The relevance of Kitamori's book to our discussion seems to me two-fold: firstly, to argue that pain should not be understood as only physical, but that it also has psychological and spiritual dimensions; pain involves the whole person. Secondly, Kitamori sees pain as essentially relational rather than exclusively individual. On a divine level, the Father suffers pain as a result of the suffering of the Son; on the human level "the pain of God gives meaning and value to human suffering" as well.[123]

Probably no one has explored this kind of relationship as deeply as Abraham Heschel in his seminal work on the Hebrew prophets.[124] Heschel's central thesis is what he terms the *pathos* of God. Pathos is for him a theological category which "gives genuine insight into God's relatedness to man". God's pathos is "his essence" and a "necessary attribute of God", which is not absolute but takes the form of his relationship with humanity, "God's participation in the predicament of me".[125] Consequently "God does not stand outside of human suffering and sorrow", but is personally involved in it because he involves himself intimately in humankind's history.[126] The thrust of Heschel's argument here is mainly of the national suffering of ancient Israel, and others who have pursued the idea of the "pain of God" have more often applied it primarily to liberation and political issues.[127] But Heschel also sees pathos in relation to the individual: "the ultimate element in the object of theological reflection", he writes, "is a transcendent divine attention to man, that man is apprehended by God".[128] The relational aspect of pain will be considered in the following chapter.

How does this discussion relate to individual suffering, and especially to pain which may be felt in approaching death? For most Christians, I suggest, the idea that God is impassible, immune from what we perceive as the emotion of pain, will be incomprehensible. Clearly God does not suffer physically, though Christians might see in the crucifixion the suffering of God in human form. To speak of the pain of God is in a sense (like much of theology) to speak in metaphors, though both Kitamori and Heschel would go beyond this and see pain as part of the essential nature of God. The question is not so much, Does God suffer? as whether pain is appropriate language to speak of God in relation to mankind. I think most believers assume that, on the basis of experience, it is. Dietrich Bonhoeffer's "only the suffering God can help" has a resonance which the traditional concept of the impassibility of God entirely lacks. Archbishop William Temple indeed argued that, "only a God in whose perfect Being pain has its place can win and hold our worship; for otherwise the creature would in fortitude surpass the Creator".[129] It is true that some have found strength to cope with pain by contemplation of the physical sufferings of Jesus and for this there is some biblical warrant (e.g. 1 Peter 4:12ff.). It is also true that the crucifixion has inspired much great art, choral music, and poetry which might inspire those in pain, especially perhaps the pains of dying. But this is not to argue, as Christians have sometimes done, that pain and suffering are meant to bring us nearer to God.[130] This may be true of some saintly souls, and some throughout Christian history have even practised self-inflicted pain as a spiritual discipline. But for others, physical or mental pain can equally lead to alienation and be destructive of faith. To regard pain as altogether beneficial is misleading and perhaps indicative that those who hold such views fail to appreciate adequately how pain is felt by others. Extreme pain is a blunt instrument and few of us can really know how it will affect us as individuals.

Both Kitamori and Heschel move us away from thinking of pain as entirely physical. Of course, the process of dying, whether long or short, may well involve physical suffering, but there is also another, and perhaps more important, dimension to pain, which one might call psychological or spiritual. I have suggested that it was this, rather than the purely physical suffering, which was behind the cry of dereliction on the cross. It is also apparent in the account of the prayer in Gethsemane in which Jesus contemplates his approaching death. In Luke's account Jesus "being in an agony . . . his sweat became as it were great drops of blood falling down to the ground" (Luke 22:44). The psychological and spiritual pains of an expected impending death have perhaps nowhere been better explored than in Donne's *Devotions upon Emergent Occasions,* composed during a serious life-threatening illness in 1623,[131] and this series of meditations is probably the fullest stage-by-stage analysis of the pains of dying in all literature.[132] Donne's dilemma is that "we cannot enjoy death because we die in this torment of sickness" for "we cannot stay till the torment come, but pre-apprehensions and presages, prophesy those torments, which induce that death before either come".[133] For him it is not so much the actual point of death and what comes after that is problematic, but rather the ill health which precedes it, and the fear of suffering pain before the end comes. Thus when we hear the church bell tolling to mark the funeral of another—"I know him, he was my neighbour"—"never send to know for whom the bell tolls; it tolls for thee".[134] Donne, I think, puts his finger on what we are apprehensive about: it not so much the fact of dying, but rather the awareness that the process of dying, especially if it is prolonged, may involve pain, indignity and the loss of physical and mental faculties. "The sense of death is most in apprehension."[135]

Donne, of course, did recover and lived another eight years of productive writing. But this brief excursus into the theological questions surrounding pain leads us to the question of whether the pain of the dying process is inevitable, whether it can be ameliorated, or whether it is legitimate to avoid it altogether by hastening death—that is, by assisted dying.

Pain and assisted dying

One of the first philosophical defences of suicide was by the eighteenth-century Scottish empiricist David Hume. Though Hume was a sceptic, in his essay *Of Suicide* he seeks to show that suicide is permissible even from a religious point of view.[136] His argument was basically twofold: firstly, that the ability to take one's own life (which is not shared by any other creature) is part of the fundamental humanity which believers would regard as given by God. Secondly, that suicide is permissible when I no longer have the power to benefit society but rather have become a burden to it. He argues that if life has become such that age, illness and misfortune make life a worse burden than death, then the individual has the right to end it. If pain and loss of hope make my life unbearable, then why should I prolong it?[137] A contemporary theologian has put the case even more bluntly: "the fight for life is meaningful as long as healing is possible, but a fight against death at any price is nonsensical: it is a help which becomes a torment".[138] A majority of church leaders, and probably a substantial percentage of medical practitioners,[139] would probably disagree with Küng. What then are the arguments for prolonging life, even when the patient is in pain and distress and nearing death, and has expressly decided to embrace assisted dying?

Some of the most important issues have been discussed earlier—the question of human autonomy, that it is against the will of God to hasten death, and that it is "not in the best interests of the patient". The

slippery-slope argument, that to allow assisted dying would inevitably result in pressure being put on the elderly to end their lives, will be considered in the following chapter. Most opponents of assisted suicide would point to the role of palliative care which, it is claimed, can make the dying process less painful, more bearable, and more dignified. Wyatt even asserts that today "it is not primarily about physical pain", and that "most people" (?) accept that "with expert palliative care pain can be reduced and controlled, if not completely eliminated", and he believes this includes "psychological pain, relational pain, and the spiritual pain so often experienced by dying people".[140] However, given that pain is experienced by each one of us in different intensities, it is hard to be confident how a physician, however empathetic, can make such a bold claim. Pain is intensely personal to the patient: the doctor can only observe and assess, not experience the patient's pain.

It is, of course, undeniable that immense improvements have been made over the last decades in mitigating the pain of the dying. The primary impetus probably came in the late 1960s through the vision of Dame Cicely Saunders, whose mission was not simply to prolong the lives of the dying and terminally ill but also to improve their quality of life. She opened the first hospice to provide this care. Today, Hospice UK is an umbrella organization for the two hundred or so hospices throughout the country. It works closely with the NHS, but is not integrated within it. Hospices are not simply places for the terminally ill, but also work with the NHS and other charitable organizations to provide support for those who wish to die at home.[141] Hospices, as charitable institutions, receive only about a third of their funding through the NHS. The estimated annual amount needed to sustain them is in the region of £1.5 billion, and so they are heavily dependent on fundraising and charitable giving. The aim of the hospice movement, in accordance with Saunders' original vision, is to care for the whole person, and to try to address the full spectrum of the needs of the terminally ill, physical, psychological and spiritual.

Palliative care as a specialism has become more prominent among medical professionals since the 1980s. Kathryn Mannix's *With the End in Mind: Dying, Death and Wisdom in an Age of Denial*[142] is an immensely moving account of her experiences as a medic and a cognitive therapist.

She argues that along with the purely medical treatment of the dying palliative care aims to provide solace and empathy. This may include assisting them to put their affairs in order to have the comfort of not leaving grieving relatives with additional burdens, and also planning their own funeral arrangements.[143] More important is seeking to uncover and provide the facilities for what is really important to them—a kind of bucket list of what is in their capacity still to enjoy.[144] Through such care the last days, though full of regrets at leaving loved ones, may not only become more bearable, but may also in some sense be experienced as the fulfilment of the life lived.

Palliative care has done immense good for those who are able to benefit from it, and as the number of professionals engaged in it increases, one hopes that such intimate personal involvement with the patient can be expanded. Palliative care, however, faces serious difficulties. The most obvious is that of funding such a high standard of before-death care. The number who at present benefit from hospice care is relatively small in comparison with a rapidly increasing ageing population. The NHS (which absorbs at present 38 per cent of all public service spending) is unable to fund it in full. Increasing demands are being placed on NHS budgets, and NICE is already unable to approve spending on drugs which would benefit young people with very rare, but treatable, illnesses. The NHS has long-term plans for a bigger focus on community care and training workers in the palliative care sector. This is laudable, but it is very doubtful whether adequate funding will materialize in the foreseeable future. This raises the serious moral problem of whether limited funding should give priority to younger patients, especially children, who could have a fuller life before them, rather than on geriatric care for those who have limited time to live.[145] Mannix sadly admits that "sometimes they live too long",[146] and Gawande devotes a whole chapter of his book to "letting go".[147] I think that most of us who have been privileged to live to old age would prefer to direct what funding is available towards treatment for those who are on the threshold of their lives, rather than those who are at the end of life.

A second problem is that prescription of drugs for those in terminal pain depends on the use of painkillers, prominent among which are opioids,[148] and the danger of their abuse is significant.[149] Opioid consumption has a long history in Britain. Laudanum (which contained 10 per cent opium and 1 per cent morphine) was regularly taken in all classes of society in the past, and only became a drug requiring a doctor's prescription at the beginning of the twentieth century. Robert de Quincey's largely autobiographical classic *Confessions of an English Opium-Eater*, which appeared in 1821, was partly intended as a warning against the side effects of opium, which included nightmares, cramps and delusions—and death. Modern studies show that other effects of the drug may include a change in the heartbeat, agitation, dizziness, hallucinations, mood swings, loss of coordination, and issues with bladder and bowels. The NHS is currently attempting to reduce the number of patients regularly taking opioids (apparently over half a million people in the UK have been taking them for over three years, seriously risking their health).[150] The tragic irony of these figures is that medical wisdom indicates that opioids are only useful in the short term, and in most cases they cease to be effective after three months. Opioids are commonly used in palliative care for pain reduction. This is not problematic for short-term relief, but it may be for those suffering from long-term illness. If after a few months they become ineffective and side effects begin to kick in, the use of opioids will become detrimental rather than palliative. If doses are increased, it may lead to a semi-comatose state of sedation. Such a condition may be an existence but is hardly meaningful life. If ventilators or other mechanical devices are used without a confident expectation of recovery the situation is even more undesirable. Gawande cites a number of cases showing that such intensive care in terminal patients is "for most people a kind of failure", and he concludes that it has serious psychological costs for patients, their families, and their carers, the latter two groups being likely to suffer from major depression up to six months after the event.[151] Badham points out that even if pain is controlled, there may well be other distressing physical consequences of prolonged palliative care.[152] He refers to Guy Brown's book[153] and concludes that nothing can ameliorate "the slow disintegration of personhood" characteristic of prolonged terminal illness.[154] The eminent clinicians Rajesh Munglani and Arun Bhaskar have pointed out that there are occasions when the pains of the dying may be "beyond the realms of medicine", and that doctors have to accept that certain symptoms cannot be alleviated. In such cases, they believe, the law should make provision not only for the right to live, but also the right to die.[155]

Clearly palliative care has a role to play, and an important one. But it is not the panacea for all ills as some have asserted. Given the inadequacy of its provision, and the increase in the number and complex needs of the aged, it is unlikely to be sufficient even for those who wish to avail themselves of it. The dependence of hospices on donations for most of their funding also raises the question of whether the best provision might become the prerogative only of the wealthy.

It is significant that several medical writers on end-of-life care have stressed the spiritual aspect of the dying process. Mannix concludes her book with a discussion of the importance of what she terms "transcendence"—the search for a "meaning beyond and yet including myself". This, she writes, is "a metaphysical construct that is the spiritual meaning of the human being".[156] Gawande has a slightly different take on the role of transcendence.[157] Referring to Josiah Royce's book *The Philosophy of Loyalty* (published back in 1908), he asks why provision of the basic necessities of life—housing, food, and so on—so often fails to render life meaningful. Royce's answer was that to be truly human we need a loyalty to something beyond ourselves and greater than us. "The only way death is not meaningless", writes Gawande, "is to see yourself as (part of) something greater"—whether that be family, society or something else. So, he concludes that some psychologists have argued that "the existence in people of a transcendent desire to see and help other beings achieve their potential" is of paramount importance. Irene Tracey's research on practising Catholics goes beyond this. She found that faith itself may have a physical effect in engaging a neural mechanism which actually reduces the sensation of pain.[158] These findings from medical practitioners will resonate with Christians, as for many other believers. For they suggest that religious faith, perhaps more than any other "loyalty", helps to set death in a more universal context and within the orbit of the love of God which can give a depth of meaning both to end-of-life suffering and death itself.

In the light of these considerations, the question of the legitimacy of provision for assisted dying becomes of crucial importance, not simply as a medical decision, but even more as a moral choice and, as importantly, a matter of simple human compassion for the dying. This will be the subject of the next chapter.

4

The eternal reciprocity of tears[159]

What is compassion?

Tolstoy's novella *The Death of Ivan Ilyich* is a profound study of the psychology of the sad process of dying. It is not that Ivan is a particularly likeable character: he is a very ordinary man with very ordinary faults, and with no exceptional gifts or moral qualities. Even the exact nature of his terminal illness is not specified. But Tolstoy's description of Ivan's long-drawn-out decline engages the reader's sympathy. It begins with an apparently trivial injury, followed by a growing awareness of its seriousness, inescapable and increasing pain, dark thoughts of death, and a final three days of screaming agony, before a final moment of peace and light. The friends and family around him (aside from his young son) are exposed in all their self-absorption, pretentiousness and hypocrisy, especially in the lie of refusing to admit to him openly that he is fast approaching the end of his life. His doctors (for whom Tolstoy shows characteristic ironic contempt) are no better. Compassion for Ivan Ilyich comes from a very unexpected source: from his peasant servant Gerasim, who is all but invisible until late in the narrative when Ivan has declined so much as to be incapable of looking after himself. In contrast to Ivan's family, Gerasim has a simple, unsophisticated acceptance of his master's condition, performing willingly the most menial and demeaning tasks for him: he is the one person who shows he understands and accepts that Ivan's illness is terminal, and treats him, despite the vast difference in their social status, as a fellow human being. Only Gerasim shows true compassion, honest empathy with Ivan's suffering, and treats him with practical good will.[160]

Tolstoy was, of course, a man well acquainted with death. Earlier in his life he had witnessed colleagues slaughtered on the battlefield; within the space of two short years he had lost five close family members, and he saw five of his own children die in childhood. It is not surprising then that at one stage in his life he had become obsessed with death, and that the fact of dying features often in his works. Though Tolstoy's faith was at odds with the Orthodox Church (which eventually excommunicated him) his description of Gerasim's relationship with Ivan is instructive for the meaning of Christian compassion. This relationship becomes deeply personal in a way which almost eclipses the social gulf between him, a peasant servant, and his master. Gerasim has a genuine understanding of the dying Ivan which enables him to "feel with" Ivan. He recognizes not only Ivan's physical pain, but also comprehends the mental torture he is experiencing. In simple honesty he acknowledges openly that Ivan is dying: to pretend that his master's illness is nothing serious (as Ivan's wife and daughter do) simply does not enter into his mind. His compassion issues in practical service which goes beyond their social relationship as servant to master. As Ivan's terminal suffering and weakness progresses, Gerasim performs even the most unpleasant tasks (a fact recognized by Ivan) with a willingness which seeks to preserve Ivan's dignity. It is "loving your neighbour as yourself", seeing the matter from the other's point of view and actively entering into his pain.

Compassion has a fundamental role in the Bible. It has its basis in the often repeated phrase that God is a compassionate God, who has loving kindness as his character.[161] It is significant that the two Hebrew words usually translated as "compassion" or "compassionate" both have their roots in organs of the physical body: compassion is, as it were, something that the body feels with a deep-seated emotion which promises loving action. The predominant term used in the Hebrew Bible is *rachum*. The word is derived from *rechem/racham* which literally means the womb. Compassion is therefore compared to the deep feeling of protection for the unborn child. The prophets often use another term also, *me'im*, which has a similar meaning of the intestines, belly (rendered in the AV as "bowels") as the seat of the emotions (Isaiah 16:11 and 63:15; Jeremiah 11:20 and 4:9; Genesis 43:30), and which can also be used in the sense of the womb or loins (Isaiah 48:19). The New Testament takes up the same imagery. To have compassion is *splagchnizo*, deriving from the *splagchna*, the inward parts, intestines, again used metaphorically of the location of feelings.[162] Paul uses this word to describe the loving affection between Christians (2 Corinthians 6:12; Philippians 1:8 and 2:1), and also in his command for compassion to others (Colossians 3:12). Its most widespread use (in the verbal form) is in the Synoptic Gospels, meaning "to have compassion on someone". It describes Jesus' compassion for the bewildered crowds (Matthew 9:36; Mark 6:34), and also for individuals (Mark 1:41; Luke 7:13). Luke uses the word of the Samaritan's compassion for the wounded victim and of the father's welcome to his erring son (Luke 10:33 and 15:20). In Matthew it is used of mutual forgiveness (18:27). Compassion in this sense may be said to lie at the heart of Jesus' message.[163]

Compassion and assisted dying

How may this inform our understanding of compassion in the context of assisted dying? Fundamentally compassion is a close personal relationship between two (or more) individuals. It is, in Martin Buber's famous terminology, an "I–Thou" relationship between the suffering person and another.[164] If we are to take the biblical material seriously, it is a deeply felt, almost bodily reaction, intense but at the same time controlled. It is more than pity, and much more than simply a detached analysis of the sufferer's condition, it is "more than feeling, a way of being (and) living with another person"[165] and seeking to enter into his or her experience; as far as is possible, it is a self-identification on the basis of a common humanity. As Donne puts it: "Any man's death diminishes me because I am involved in mankind (and) all mankind is of one author",[166] since all derive their lives from God. Or more prosaically, as a consultant once put it to me, "I am a person before I am a doctor".

Perhaps it is for this reason that dying alone without compassionate companionship is something which many people fear—though of course for the Christian no one dies without the presence of God. Sociologists have pointed to a situation which has become all too common in modern Western societies, the "social death" which may precede physical death.

For an increasing number of the elderly, circumstances may make it all but impossible to engage with their communities to any significant degree. Illness, infirmity, and lack of mobility are significant factors which lead to social isolation. This has become an increasing dilemma for many, with the loosening of family and neighbourhood ties, and often the physical distance between family members. The psychological impact resulting from such loneliness may exacerbate physical decline.[167] As one poet has put it: "Before you lie down, Ready for the last night, You must taste the dry rusk, Of being excluded."[168] True compassion for the dying is not confined to the last moments but begins with the loneliness that frequently precedes it.

Is compassion compatible with assisted dying? Opponents of assisted dying assert that it is not and maintain that the only compassionate response to painful terminal illness is by palliative care. We have discussed the problems of this stance in the previous chapter. I believe that in some cases prolonging life by palliative care could be the least compassionate possible course to take. If death is inevitable in the longer or shorter run for the patient, as it is for all of us at some point, if there is no realistic hope for return to a reasonable quality of life, and if the patient wishes to be released from pain, then surely a dignified passing through assisted dying is the more compassionate option. It is frequently remarked that we act more compassionately by "putting down" an animal with an incurable condition, but deny a similar death to fellow humans. Sometimes death is the preferable option to a life of unendurable pain. A former colleague, whose wife died of a heart attack, which, had she survived, would have left her very seriously disabled, once remarked to me that she would greatly have preferred to die rather than live in such a condition. I think this might resonate with many of us: what we fear most is not so much death itself, as the loss of our personhood which may deprive us of meaningful life even while we still breathe. The knowledge that there can be a way out through assisted dying can be a comfort to those suffering painful illness, and an encouragement to face life for the moment.[169] But for some the timing of an assisted dying is made more problematic by the current law in the UK. For someone suffering the creeping deterioration of a disease, like muscular dystrophy, the present law which criminalizes those who assist suicide presents an insoluble dilemma: should I travel to Switzerland or elsewhere to avail myself of assisted dying now, when I still have the physical capacity and some reasonable quality of life, or should I delay it and risk not being well enough to travel unaided—in which case anyone who assists me will be liable to criminal prosecution? As we shall see in chapter 6, several cases have come before the law courts to petition for immunity from prosecution for assisters, but the courts have had little alternative but to uphold the law as it stands. There is a similar dilemma with advanced treatment declarations (living wills). These at the moment can only legally instruct on refusal of medical care should a person become so incapacitated in the future as to be unable to make a decision. However, it is quite clear that there are those who would prefer to opt for assisted dying rather than live with conditions which, for them, would render continued life meaningless. This is perhaps especially the case for those who have been diagnosed with an advancing mental affliction like Alzheimer's disease. I think that for many of us the prospect of being so debilitated as to be unable even to recognize and communicate with those whom we love would constitute a loss of any meaningful sense of personhood. To be able to make an advanced decision opting for assisted dying in such an eventuality would be for many a considerable comfort. Situations of this kind are, it seems to me, strong arguments for legalizing assisted dying in the UK on compassionate grounds. But perhaps we should put the question of compassion in a different way: is it compassionate, or indeed moral, to prolong life which is not any longer the *real* life which the sufferer wants—"as tho' to breathe were life"?[170] As Holloway remarks: "The karma of modern medicine keeps too many people alive long after any pleasure or meaning has gone from their lives. Sentenced to years of mournful dissolution, many of them long to be blown out like a candle."[171] The choice is between two outcomes, both of which are to some degree undesirable. But to the Christian, death, as we shall argue in chapter 6, will be the entrance into a fuller form of life. And as Holloway has it, why should those who do not believe in afterlife have any fear of dying?[172]

Assisted dying does not imply, as Wyatt asserts, "it is bad for you to live".[173] Rather it echoes the words of Ecclesiastes that "there is a time to die", a time for our three score years and ten—or whatever it may be for each one of us—to come to a close. In 2015, the Royal College of Physicians

(RCP) acknowledged that "thousands of us die badly" in NHS hospitals (quite apart from elsewhere). This is not compassion. Compassion is better exercised allowing those suffering from extreme pain and terminal illness to have a dignified release. As Badham argues, "To insist that people should put up with suffering that they find unbearable during the dying process seems strange if one takes the Christian hope for the afterlife seriously."[174]

Considering others

Is assisted dying a selfish act which can have grievous consequences for other people? Those most likely to be affected are those we leave behind, family and friends. The question that needs to be addressed is not strictly, "how will my death affect those I love?" We all, of course, have to face bereavement some time, so the fact of the death of someone close to you, when the physical relationship is terminated, is an unavoidable reality, whether by natural causes or not. The question is rather whether there will be additional grief caused by the choice to utilize assisted dying, hastening death, but at the same time shortening the dying process. This is perhaps a question which no one can really solve for another. But for some the distress of witnessing a long-drawn-out process of letting a terminal illness move towards its inevitable end, with all the pain and humiliating dependence on others, may be additional grief to the actual passing itself. And most of us, I imagine, would prefer not to be remembered in our last days in that way. Hamlet's profound mixed metaphors as he contemplated suicide speak equally to the case of assisted dying:

> Whether 'tis nobler in the mind to suffer
> The slings and arrows of outrageous fortune,
> Or to take arms against a sea of troubles,
> And by opposing end them? To die, to sleep.[175]

We are faced with alternatives in considering the mourners: whether to fight against our mortality to the bitter end or embrace what seems to be the right time to die. We cannot spare those we leave from the fact of death, but the option for assisted dying might well spare them from the distress of witnessing a prolonged and painful path to dying.

But there is another side to the relationship between the terminally ill person and his or her carers, the impact that prolonged caring for someone has on them. Research conducted by the Universities of Birmingham and Sheffield in 2019 found that half of all women will be carers by the age of forty-six, and half of men by the age of fifty-seven. It further estimated that two thirds of adults can expect to become unpaid carers during their lifetime.[176] According to the Carers Trust, there are some seven million carers throughout the UK. An even more worrying factor is the number of children, some of only primary school age, who care for chronically ill parents.[177] Adult carers may have to give up their employment or work part-time, have drastically reduced social interaction, and may hardly have a fulfilled life of their own. However much love and affection there may be between the carer and the cared for, these are enormous physical and psychological, and often financial, burdens unpaid family carers are expected to carry. And in some—perhaps many—cases the terminally ill themselves would favour release by assisted dying. A survey, also in 2019, of 502 patients with terminal illnesses found that around two thirds would welcome the opportunity to avail themselves of assisted dying.[178] This seems to reflect a fairly commonly held view among the elderly, especially the terminally ill, that they do not wish to become such a burden on their spouses or children that it would seriously disrupt the lives of their survivors.[179] It is sometimes argued that, as parents have cared for their children when young, children should reciprocate by caring for infirm parents later in life. While no one would probably want to refute this, it becomes a much more serious problem when an obligation of care for the elderly drastically affects younger folk with their lives in front of them, and whose primary responsibility is to their own children. I suppose that most of us who have reached old age would wish to see younger people have a fulfilled life: to "honour father and mother" by no means absolves us from responsibilities for the young.

It is also important that consideration is paid to the possible effect on those who will carry out assisted dying, whether—as would be usual—a medical practitioner, or some other "assister". Assisted dying will necessarily mean involvement by another, usually unrelated, person who will help end the life. This may be by a direct or an indirect act, usually involving the provision of a lethal dose of barbiturates for the person to drink by themselves.[180] Thus the medical assister will share a certain degree of responsibility. Medical opinion seems generally to be softening towards assisted dying. However, it seems to me ethically wrong to require doctors who are conscientiously not in agreement with assisted dying to act in this capacity. Experience in other countries where assisted dying is legal does not suggest that this would have a serious effect on its availability in the UK. Admittedly, our legal system is not very good at allowing exceptions for conscience's sake, but it should not be impossible in a compassionate society to make provisions for physicians to excuse themselves from a procedure about which they may have conscientious convictions.

Related to this is the objection, sometimes raised,[181] that assisted dying would be in contradiction to the Hippocratic Oath. Aside from the fact that the "Hippocratic Oath" is almost certainly not the work of the Greek physician Hippocrates (c. 460–370 BC) (though usually included in the corpus of his writings), it is somewhat bewildering that such an ancient writing should be regarded as determinative for modern medicine. Historically, of course, it did have considerable influence for the ethical practice of medicine, mainly perhaps in a later Latin form by the injunction "primarily do no harm" (*primus non nocere*).[182] As one would expect, the Hippocratic Oath has been revised frequently in modern times, most importantly by the World Medical Association in 1948 as a result of the horrors of World War II. It was revised again in the 1960s to include "the utmost respect for human life from the beginning", and more recently as a consequence of the World Health Organization's statement that climate change represented a significant threat to human health. In the UK, the role of the Hippocratic Oath has been replaced by the General Medical Council's document *Good Medical Practice*,[183] and most other countries have similar guidelines. Specifically as regards assisted dying the GMC's advice to doctors is, as one would expect, to remind doctors that respect for a patient's autonomy in requesting assisted dying cannot override the fact that it is "a criminal offence to encourage or assist a person to commit or attempt suicide". It also includes advice on end-of-life care.[184] The guidance makes no attempt to pronounce on the ethical arguments for or against assisted dying, and presumably would have to be reworded if ever assisted dying were to be made legal.

The most common, and perhaps superficially the most cogent, argument against legalizing assisted dying has been that of consideration for others, who might thereby be encouraged to end their own lives.[185] This is the so-called "slippery-slope" argument: if assisted dying is legalized, the inevitable result would be that more and more people will request it. Eventually, the argument goes, assisted dying will become a normal way to end life, and will result in younger people and many with manageable disabilities or indeed mental health afflictions requesting it. This sounds a reasonable stance, but I believe that it is simplistic and seriously exaggerated.

"Slippery-slope" arguments which seek to restrict or ban certain actions are themselves logically problematic. It has been pointed out that the argument is inherently self-contradictory, in that it is itself a slippery slope—the more it is appealed to the more likely is it to result in encouraging the banning of more and more actions, many of which will be quite harmless in themselves. It argues that actions which *may* have a pejorative effect should be disallowed. In fact, the medical profession itself does not follow this practice: codeine, and many other drugs, can (and do) have serious side effects (in extreme cases including death), but are not banned outright in the interests of protecting vulnerable people. Instead, their use is (increasingly in the case of codeine) strictly controlled. If the slippery-slope argument were to have any validity in respect of assisted dying, it would have to be demonstrated empirically not only that making it available would lead to an increase in the numbers of people seeking it, but it would also have to be proved that this increase was the direct result of making assisted dying legal. In the nature of the case this is virtually impossible. There are, and will continue to be, many reasons why people seek assisted dying: its influence on others taking this step *might* in some cases be an attributable cause, but aside from the fact it would be one reason among many, it would be very difficult to prove. Biggar goes to great lengths to try to demonstrate support for his slippery-slope argument against assisted dying (or assisted suicide, as he terms it) from the data from Holland up to the time of writing.

But he honestly acknowledges that other researchers, on the basis of the same figures, have come to different conclusions.[186] And, as one reviewer has pointed out, Biggar restricts himself only to the data from the Netherlands, but evidence from elsewhere (e.g. Oregon) does not support Biggar's conclusions.[187] Furthermore, the situation has moved on considerably in the last decade and a half. But, as I have suggested above, even if there is an increasing demand for assisted dying in those countries where it is legal, this by no means proves that the *cause* of this increase is due to any slippery slope.[188] Any increase in demand for assisted dying as a result of its being legalized in the UK (if that were ever to happen) would much more likely be due to the fact that, as it would no longer be a criminal act, more people would be likely to avail themselves of it. The substantial number of UK citizens travelling to Europe for assisted dying, as well as the increasing number of court cases petitioning for immunity from prosecution for those who assist, suggests that there are many who would opt for assisted dying but are deterred because of legal restrictions. As we have seen, surveys (whatever their deficiencies) by polling companies confirm this.

The slippery-slope objection is a *hypothetical* argument of the "if such . . . what then?" type. Like all hypothetical arguments it is speculative and unprovable. It is also (despite Biggar's protestations) a consequentialist one, that is, that it is the *consequences* of an act (rather than its motive) which determine whether it is ethical or not. Thus it focuses on the results of the act of assisted dying rather than on whether the act is morally justified in itself. Basically, the slippery-slope type of objection to assisted dying will only be convincing to those who are already persuaded on other grounds that assisted dying is wrong. For those who support assisted dying the argument has no force, for if I approve assisted dying for myself as a morally acceptable alternative to a painful terminal illness, then I cannot logically deny it to others. What is important in protecting vulnerable people from opting for assisted dying when the circumstances may not be right for them, is that sufficient legal and ethical guidelines are put in place to prevent its being abused. Biggar is not convinced this is possible. This seems to me unduly pessimistic. It should not be beyond the wit of the legal and medical professions, with the help of psychiatrists, clergy, and carers where appropriate, to put in place sufficient safeguards which would enable those with a genuine case and desire to avail themselves of assisted dying to do so, while at the same time separating out those cases where such an act would not be a proper course to follow. As a basic minimum such guidelines would have to include a terminal medical condition, intolerable pain experienced by the patient, mental competence, and a settled and expressed decision held over a reasonable period of time. We shall consider this question in more detail in the next chapter. But "what's best for the patient", when all these things have been properly considered, is surely best left to the patient himself or herself. In sum it seems to me that compassion will best be served by making assisted dying available to those afflicted with a debilitating illness which has no reasonable hope of an acceptable level of alleviation, and who do not wish to prolong such a painful existence.

5

Better is eternal rest than
continual sickness[189]

Between experience and the law: a dilemma

The sociologist Karl Mannheim, in the course of his critique of the baneful influence of ideologies on society, commented that the "very formation of a problem is made possible only by previous actual human experience that involves such a problem".[190] In the context of our discussion of assisted dying one might colloquially paraphrase this as "if you have never been there you will not have much idea of what it is like", that is, that those who have never experienced the dilemma of seeing a loved one die in pain are not in a good position to make a meaningful judgement on assisted dying. Archbishop George Carey, in his personal statement explaining why he changed his mind to support assisted dying, draws a contrast in approaches to the issue.[191] On the one hand there are those who claim that Christian tradition and doctrine are sharply opposed to ending life in this way. This approach is well illustrated in Biggar's strictly detached and academic attempt to deconstruct arguments which are advanced to support assisted dying.[192] On the other side are those who in one way or another have been brought face to face with (in Carey's words) "people in extreme agony, who, in their separation and misery desired a merciful release from their sufferings".[193] This is perhaps a present-day situation which mirrors the conflict we find so often in the Gospels between Jesus and those of the Pharisees who would elevate a dogmatic and uncompassionate interpretation of the demands of the religious law above the needs of the human individual.

It is surely significant that two of the earliest modern defenders of assisted dying, Küng and Badham, came to that view as a result of loved members of their families suffering horribly in the dying process. For Küng, it was witnessing the physical decline of his brother suffering from an inoperable brain cancer.[194] In Badham's case it was not only the deaths of his grandparents, but even more the extreme physical and mental distress suffered by both his parents in the process of dying.[195] These accounts are heart-rending to read, but they could be multiplied many times over, for most incidents of agonizing dying are not documented. Of course, many terminally ill people do not die in agony or even in pain. But sadly a great many more do. For such, and for those who witness their passing, Küng's question forces itself upon us, "whether this is the death that God gives, that God ordains": is it "God-given", "divinely willed", even "pleasing to God"?[196] We cannot avoid, too, asking ourselves, would not a loving and compassionate God feel the same grief as mourners do, can there not be a more peaceful and dignified release?

These questions are raised, but not answered, in the many high-profile cases involving requests for assisted dying or for immunity for those relatives and medics who may "assist".

The Suicide Act of 1961 abrogated the earlier law against suicide in a single sentence (section 1). It substituted instead the "criminal liability for complicity in another's suicide" (section 2). This offence is defined not only as encouraging or assisting the suicide of another person, but also as "intending to encourage such an act", whether or not such a suicide or attempted suicide actually takes place (2.1.B). Section 2 also includes in the offence arranging for another person to encourage or assist suicide or attempted suicide. Prosecution can only be instigated by the Director of Public Prosecutions. The penalty, if the person is found guilty, is a maximum sentence of fourteen years' imprisonment. The legislation is strict and is presumably primarily intended to prevent harm to those regarded as vulnerable, rather than to give adequate consideration to those who wish to commit suicide (no longer a crime under section 1), but are unable to do so unaided. The use of the word "intention" is particularly problematic: intentions are personal and internal, and it is hard to see how they could be proved without a shadow of doubt in a court of law. A frank discussion about assisted dying with a suffering relative could in some circumstances fall foul of this legislation, so the law as it stands can well have the effect of shutting down discussion of the dying process. Potentially, in a hostile court, even raising the subject with one suffering from terminal illness could land one in prison for fourteen years.[197] The problems with the 1961 Act have been reflected in the low number of cases which come to court. The Crown Prosecution Service (CPS) reports that between April 2009 and July 2019 there were 152 cases referred to them by the police. Of these 104 were not taken further, and twenty-nine were later withdrawn by the police. Of the remainder, three cases were successfully prosecuted, in one of which the accused was acquitted; a further eight were upgraded to charges of homicide. Defenders of the Act might argue from the miniscule number of convictions that the Act is working as a deterrent. However, the large number of legal challenges to it suggests a very different conclusion.

The first significant attempt to challenge the 1961 Act was by Diane Pretty in 2002. Mrs Pretty, a mother of two, suffered from progressive and incurable motor neurone disease. She petitioned for a guarantee that her husband would not face prosecution if he should in the future help her die. This was rejected by the House of Lords.[198] Their reasoning was that the constitutional "right to life" did not include a "right to die". The European Court of Human Rights agreed with this judgement and concluded that the right to life was not determined by *quality* of life, and therefore could not be construed as bestowing the right to die. However, it then went on to state that Mrs Pretty's right to die did come under the "respect for a private life" under section 8 of the Human Rights Act 1998, but it qualified this by upholding the validity of the 1961 Act on assisted suicide in the UK. Such prevarication might well seem to be a piece of legal casuistry rather than basic common sense.[199] The case brought by Debbie Purdy involved a judicial review in 2008 and concluded with a judgement in the House of Lords in July 2009.[200] Purdy had been diagnosed with progressive and incurable multiple sclerosis in 1995, and when the judicial review began she was confined to a wheelchair, had severely limited ability to carry out basic tasks, and had choking fits and difficulties in swallowing, all of which, according to her lawyer, would eventually "render her continuing existence no longer of an acceptable quality". She had determined that when her condition became unbearable, she would travel to Switzerland to avail herself of assisted dying. To do this she would require the help of her husband Omar Puente. She therefore sought a judicial review challenging the Director of Public Prosecutions (DPP) to publish details of its policy in relation to offences deemed to be committed under the 1961 Act, section 2. Unlike the Pretty case, Ms Purdy was not appealing for immunity for her "assister" but for clarification of the criteria the DPP would use in pursuance of any prosecution. Her view was that the law was unclear. The Court of Appeal expressed its sympathy, but accepted the Lords' ruling in the Pretty case that, under the Human Rights Act, section 8, the right to life did not include the right to decide when and how to die. When the case came before the House of Lords they surprisingly disagreed with the decision made by the Law Lords in the Pretty case. In the words of Debbie Purdy's lawyer, Saimo Chahal: "in a unanimous judgement in favour of Ms Purdy (they) said that the House was free to depart from its earlier decision in *Pretty*. They said the present law does interfere with Ms Purdy's right to respect for private life. She has the right to determine how to spend the closing moments of her life, which is part of the act of living. Ms Purdy wishes to avoid an undignified and distressing end to her life. This should be respected." Consequently, the Lords required the DPP to prepare an "offence-specific" policy statement showing the circumstances in which it would or would not prosecute under the Act. They also criticized the CPS for lack of guidance on the issue. As a result, a consultation was initiated that same year.[201] The CPS issued detailed advice in the following year, and again in 2014. It is unnecessary to review these guidelines in detail here, which in any case did little to lessen opposition to the Act. The main fact is that the Act has caused considerable confusion and controversy, not only among the general public but also for the police and legal profession. This confusion is well illustrated by the case of Mavis Eccleston. Mrs Eccleston, at the age of eighty, was charged with the murder and manslaughter of her husband Denis, who was suffering from terminal cancer, by giving him a potentially lethal dose of prescription drugs: she herself then also took an overdose in what was clearly intended to be a suicide pact. Both were discovered unconscious and rushed to hospital, but only Mrs Eccleston survived. In a trial in 2018, the prosecution contended she had administered the medicine to her husband without his consent, despite the fact that she clearly stated she had acted in accordance with his wishes. Mrs Eccleston was arrested, detained for thirty hours, and charged with murder and manslaughter. At her trial at Stafford Crown Court she was found not guilty by the jury and acquitted. Her daughter later called for the law to be changed, "so that people who are dying are not forced to suffer, making plans in secret, or ask loved ones to risk prosecution by helping them". The CPS claimed that prosecution was "in the public interest", but even the anti-euthanasia lobby group Care Not Killing admitted that "this troubling case . . . should never have come to court".[202] Fortunately in this case common sense prevailed because of the compassionate understanding of the members of the jury.

There have been numerous other cases in which the police have engaged in inquiries resulting from allegations (often resulting from anonymous tip-offs) of assisting suicide, some of which have caused great distress to elderly bereaved relatives. George Whaley, an eighty-year-old suffering from motor neurone disease, made his own arrangements to end his life at Dignitas. Before he and his wife left, both were interviewed by Thames Valley Police, his wife Ann twice, under caution. They travelled to Switzerland in February 2019. Two months later the case took a significant turn, when Ann Whaley attended a Reith Lecture given by Lord Sumption QC. Sumption is a former member of the Supreme Court. Ann questioned Lord Sumption on the assisted dying law after his lecture. His reply was surprising and, to the non-legal mind, somewhat puzzling: "I think that the law should continue to criminalize assisted suicide, and I think that the law should be broken from time to time." He went on: "We need to have a law against it in order to prevent abuse . . . but it's also been the case that courageous friends and families have helped people to die. I don't believe there's a moral obligation to obey the law. Ultimately it's for each person to decide."[203] It is scarcely surprising that Mrs Whaley should have commented that this indicated that Sumption was "completely ignorant of the reality faced by dying people and their loved ones".[204] At the same time it suggests an extraordinary lack of logical thinking: if Sumption considered the law to be just, then it is reprehensible of him to suggest that people should break it; if he considers it unjust, he should surely be supporting a change. It is precisely such lack of clarity, especially with regard to the process and reasoning behind criteria for prosecution, which needs addressing. The present scattergun approach to enforcing this law is hopelessly confusing and serves as no sensible guidance for those caught up in the dilemma of assisted dying.

Police investigation and a possible criminal charge are not the only threats spouses have to face when accused under the assisted suicide legislation. In 2017, Alexander Ninian, who was suffering from terminal supranuclear palsy, decided to end his life at Dignitas. Though his wife, Sarah, did not agree with his decision, she nevertheless chose to accompany him even though she knew she might face prosecution. On her return the CPS decided it was not in the public interest to prosecute, but she faced being debarred from inheriting her late husband's estate under the Forfeiture Act of 1982.[205] She was obliged to make a very expensive application to the High Court to request this penalty be waived.

It should be stressed that the police themselves are put into difficulties by the assisted suicide legislation. While they are obliged to investigate, police questioning of those who are vulnerable, and may also be suffering bereavement, may be experienced as unsympathetic harassment. There is increasing evidence that the police themselves are uneasy with the present position. According to Dignity in Dying some eighteen police and crime commissioners have now requested the Secretary of State for Justice to initiate an inquiry into the law as it currently stands.[206]

The Pretty and Purdy cases were followed by several other appeals to the courts. Two of these have relevance to the subject of this book. The Tony Nicklinson case began in 2010.[207] Nicklinson suffered from locked-in syndrome as a result of a stroke that left him unable to move and only able to communicate through a specially adapted computer. His petition was for a change in the law which would afford him assistance to die (which of course he was not able to do by himself) and for immunity for the doctor who administered the fatal medicine. His solicitor (also Saimo Chahal) argued that the law on assisted suicide infringed his right to a private life under the European Convention on Human Rights. The Supreme Court refused his application in 2014. Its reasoning was that a change in the law was beyond the remit of the courts and could only be enacted by Parliament, and then not on the basis of individual cases.[208] Mr Nicklinson died just a week later aged fifty-eight. His solicitor stated that he was "devastated and frightened" at the rejection of his case and had refused food before his death. This case effectively shut off appeals to the European Convention on Human Rights.

The case of Phil Newby in 2019 raised a wider and more fundamental moral issue, namely what is a "civilized" ending to life? His petition proposed that the judges should carefully look at the expert evidence, which would include that from countries where assisted dying is legal, to consider whether the current law is compatible with basic human rights. The High Court, having expressed the routine sympathy with the applicant, predictably concluded that the court was not the right body for a consideration of what it called "the sanctity of life". The most remarkable submission in this case was the argument presented by the lawyers for the Ministry of Justice. Their contention was that it is already legal for a person to take his or her own life by starving himself to death—"the law does not prevent a person from acting autonomously in his own capacity in refusing life-sustaining nutrition, hydration or treatment". Unsurprisingly, Mr Newby's wife, Charlotte, is reported to have commented to Sky News, "I think that's an utterly shocking thing to say to somebody—you can starve yourself to death and refuse water and that's solved the problem".[209] However, perhaps Mrs Newby should not have been surprised, though she had every reason to be outraged. Almost incredible as it may seem to the lay person, such a course of action has at times been advocated by the NHS itself. What became known as the "Liverpool Care Pathway"[210] was a programme intended to give healthcare staff guidance to improve care in the final days of a person's life, to bring about a comfortable death, and was intended to be "a model of excellence". One advocate of the pathway subsequently claimed, in its defence, that the Liverpool Care Pathway had actually "been standard practice in a number of hospitals for a number of years".[211] On the one hand it sensibly advised against over-treatment of the terminally ill; on the other it recommended consideration of the withdrawal of artificial feeding and hydration from them. It is scarcely surprising that the Liverpool Care Pathway raised very considerable public and media controversy. Among the objections were complaints that relatives were not consulted about decisions to put patients on the pathway and especially that thirsty patients had effectively been denied water. As a result it was subject to a review, subsequently discontinued, and new guidelines issued by NICE.[212] However, these too were vigorously opposed, including by some eminent medical practitioners, both on the grounds that the guidelines continued to approve withdrawal of hydration and also due to concern over misleading and questionable criteria for diagnosis.[213] In effect, the Liverpool Care Pathway is euthanasia in all but name. The only reasonable conclusion one can draw is that the NHS and NICE are more than a little confused about what to do with those who suffer in the latter stages of terminal illness.

By and large the official attitude of the NHS, as with the courts, has been to uphold section 2 of the Suicide Act of 1961, that positive action to bring about death is not legally acceptable. However, there appears to be yet another routine exception to this rule. NHS guidelines do not show the same enthusiasm for preserving the lives of seriously impaired infants. Though this subject is not strictly parallel to assisted dying, it does further illustrate the confusion, indeed the contradictory nature, of present law and medical practice. There have recently been several cases of the courts refusing to allow the parents of seriously ill children either to continue their lives by life-support technology or, more surprisingly, to allow them to be transferred outside the UK for treatment of one kind or another. The case of Charlie Gard in 2017 was one which raised a public outcry and worldwide attention, even receiving the support of the Pope and President Donald Trump. Charlie, although apparently not disabled at birth, quickly developed a very rare condition which left him severely brain-damaged, partially paralysed, and unable to breathe unaided. His parents wanted him to be treated in America and raised over a million pounds for this purpose. Protracted court procedures meant his condition continued to deteriorate and the judge finally acceded to the request of Great Ormond Street Hospital that his life-support machine should be switched off. He died just short of his first birthday. It was reported that the NHS had spent nearly half a million pounds in legal fees.[214] Another high-profile case, that of Alfie Evans, in the following year was similar. Alfie suffered from a brain condition which doctors in Alder Hey Hospital in Liverpool could neither identify nor cure. His parents disagreed with the hospital's decision to stop life support. The Bambino Gesu Hospital in Italy, though not professing to be able to cure him, offered to continue the life support. Alder Hey Hospital, however, went to the High Court arguing this course of action was "not in his best interest". The High Court and subsequently the Court of Appeal and Supreme Court confirmed this judgement. Alfie died a month before his second birthday.[215] In these cases (and others like them) the courts have effectively sanctioned "passive" euthanasia. But if, as I have argued above, the distinction between passive and active euthanasia made by the medical institutions (not by the law) is without meaning, these judgements sit very uncomfortably with the criminalizing of assisted dying. Both these cases, like assisted dying, raise the question of who precisely should decide "what is in the patient's best interest"—should medical professionals or judges have the right and power to overrule the wishes of the individual or, in the case of infants, the parents? Corinne Yates, Charlie Gard's mother, has advocated setting up a committee of concerned parties to address the question of "best interests", and to remove the decision-making from the courts.[216] This would surely be a positive step. I have referred to these cases of young children neither to support nor to deny the right of "pulling the plug", that is, discontinuing life support, but rather to illustrate the complexity—indeed the contradictory nature—of decisions made under the present law.

The law against assisted dying cannot reasonably be claimed to have sufficient clarity or to have worked well. As Lord Falconer, a Labour peer and former Lord Chancellor, in his briefing paper on his own proposals for change characterized it, the Suicide Act as it stands is "an incoherent, cruel, and hypocritical mess".[217] There are at least three areas in which it singularly fails properly to address the needs of those who face the dilemma of a life of continual pain with no prospect of improvement. These issues have been explored in chapters 2, 3 and 4 above, and are not only moral issues but also fundamental theological ones. The law is theologically flawed in that it sets aside God-given human autonomy, takes no cognisance of a God who in his pain feels our pain, and who in his compassion demands compassion in us.

Seeking a better way

It is not surprising, then, that there have been several attempts in the past decades to change the law on assisted suicide. The first serious attempt was by Lord Joffe. His bill received a second reading in the House of Lords in 2003 but ran out of time. It was reintroduced the following year and referred to a select committee. It was brought down on the second reading in 2006. In Scotland a similar proposal was introduced by an MSP (who himself was suffering from terminal illness) which would have allowed those who suffered from life-limiting or life-shortening conditions to be prescribed lethal medicine by a doctor. It came before the Scottish Parliament in 2015 (after the death of its original proposer) but was defeated. In 2013, Lord Falconer introduced his Assisted Dying Bill in the House of Lords. It was largely based on the Oregon Death and Dignity Act which had been approved by that state as long ago as 1997. This passed on second reading, and with amendments was passed unanimously by the Lords. Attempts made early in 2015 to wreck the bill by further amendments were comprehensively defeated. However, as a general election was held in the May of that year the bill ran out of time. Falconer's bill received open support from outside the UK from Archbishop Emeritus Desmond Tutu, writing in a forthright article published in *The Guardian*.[218] What had been a domestic debate had now attracted serious worldwide media attention. The Assisted Dying Bill came before the newly elected House of Commons in September 2015 as a private member's bill introduced by the Labour MP Rob Marris. After a passionate debate it was defeated by the large majority of 330 votes to 118. Prime Minister David Cameron had previously indicated that he would oppose the bill. This would seriously have limited the time to consider it, since it was a private member's bill not a government-sponsored one. One former cabinet minister (whose parents had died from cancer) subsequently berated what he called the "Catholic and faith lobby" for limiting personal autonomy.[219] This reflected the widespread opinion that the institutional opposition of the churches to assisted dying had played a significant role in the defeat of the bill.

Falconer's proposals were, in fact, quite robust in defining the conditions under which assisted dying would be legal, and it will be helpful to consider these in a little more detail. Assisted dying would only be available to persons over eighteen years of age who had lived in the UK for at least a year. The bill required that those wishing to avail themselves of assisted dying should demonstrate a "settled intention" to end their lives. They would have to make a declaration to that effect, and this had to be countersigned by the registered medical practitioner whom the applicant had requested to assist them and also by a second independent doctor unconnected with that medical practitioner. Both doctors who signed the declaration were required to be satisfied that the patient was terminally ill and reasonably expected to die within six months. They further needed to assure themselves that the patient "has a clear and settled intention to end their own life, which has been reached voluntarily on an informed basis and without duress". The medicine must be self-ingested and self-administered, and the assister could only prepare the medicine and advise how it should be taken, but would not be permitted to assist physically. The bill also allowed for those doctors who had conscientious objections to assisted dying to excuse themselves from participating. To those who accept the legitimacy of assisted dying in principle these restrictions will probably seem extremely tight. They guarantee the patient is acting willingly in what he or she believes to be in their own best interests and not as a result of incitement by others. The demand for scrutiny by two medical practitioners is sensible, though in cases of serious doubt provision might perhaps have been made for further conversation with other independent persons, for example a priest, psychiatrist, or solicitor. The guidelines go as far as is possible to absolve the assisting medics from the charge of complicity in the death.

There are, however, for supporters of assisted dying, at least three potential difficulties with Falconer's bill. Perhaps the most problematic stems from the strictness of the "hands off" requirement for doctors, which would be impossible in a minority of cases. Some of the most harrowing of the appeals for assisted dying have come from those who are physically unable to self-ingest or self-administer the medicine. Falconer's bill would not have helped Tony Nicklinson or others in a similar condition to end their lives. The result would be to deny a right to the most seriously affected which would be available to those with a less debilitating condition. To be consistent and non-discriminatory provision would also have to be made for a direct intervention by the assisting person, whether a doctor or a non-medic. Another potential difficulty is the "six months to live" clause. Aside from the fact that such exact diagnoses are sometimes extremely difficult to make, this restriction would exclude those who do not have such a terminal diagnosis but nevertheless live with such life-limiting, unbearable and untreatable pain that they cannot imagine continuing to live in such a condition perhaps for decades to come. The case of the Paralympic athlete Marieke Vervoort is a moving example of this (see note 169). The Scottish proposal which spoke of "life-limiting and life-threatening" medical conditions seems to be more humane than the restriction of terminal diagnosis in Falconer's bill. Of course, objectors to assisted dying would no doubt argue that this would open the floodgates to pressure those with disabilities to end their lives. But this, I believe, is not convincing. A disability is not the same thing as a progressive illness, and the two categories should not be unjustifiably conflated; cases of disability would not pass the requirement of medical scrutiny required by Falconer. Moreover, there is no empirical evidence that legalization of assisted dying elsewhere has affected the care of the disabled. This is perhaps a variant of the "slippery-slope" argument which was discussed in the preceding chapter.

Thirdly, Falconer's insistence on mental capability raises a different and much more problematic issue. It is certainly justified in that if a patient is mentally incapacitated and unable to make his or her own decision, then it would be a violation of their personal autonomy to proceed with assisted dying—quite apart from any other moral questions such an action would involve. However, there may well be cases in which a person, suffering from a condition such as progressive dementia, might decide that at some time in the future he or she would rather end his or her life, than continue to exist in a condition under which he or she could no longer interact with family members. In such a situation it could be argued that an advance directive should be available. Such directives are already possible (though not at the moment legally binding) to refuse treatment or resuscitation in case of bodily illness.

Replacing the 1961 Suicide Act would, of course, not be easy. Lawmakers would need to be reasonably sure that permitting assisted dying within certain parameters would find sufficient support not only among the general public but also in Parliament. If recent polls are to be trusted, it is clear that a substantial majority of the population wish to see the law on assisted dying liberalized. Parliament is perhaps a different matter, though many voices critical of the present law have been raised within it. Medical opinion, too, is undergoing something of a change. I shall return to these issues in the final chapter. The task for the legal officers who draft government legislation will be to come up with a form of words which would permit those suffering unbearable pain and who wish to end their own lives to do so, while at the same time adequately protecting the potentially vulnerable. The wording would also have to give clarity to all parties charged with enforcing the law, the police and DPP, and judges and juries. To do so they will have to take a wider view, carefully considering the advice of professionals in medical and mental health, and of course the good sense of public opinion. In formulating legislation for the UK careful consideration would also need to be given to the laws in those countries which at present permit assisted dying. I believe that Christian theology, and indeed the contributions of all the religious groups in the UK, must also have an important role to play in this discussion. This may well be a tightrope for lawmakers to tread, since assisted dying involves human emotion and human compassion quite as much as the physical act of dying. But it is very clear that the Suicide Act 1961 has proved unworkable and needs to be replaced.

6

And death shall be no more;
death, thou shalt die[220]

Is belief in life after death sustainable?

If this book were written from an atheist, or even an agnostic, point of view, it would have had to end at the conclusion of the last chapter. However, a Christian, like adherents of most other religions, cannot agree with Macbeth's assertion that human

> [l]ife's but a walking shadow . . .
> That struts and frets his hour upon the stage
> And then is heard no more.

Still less could he (or she) conclude that life "is a tale told by an idiot, full of sound and fury, Signifying nothing".[221] For the earliest Christians death was most definitely not the end, but the entrance into a different dimension of existence, variously described as everlasting life, the life of the world to come, or (as the Book of Common Prayer has it) "the sure and certain hope of the resurrection to eternal life".

Almost all civilizations have held that there is some kind of afterlife. For eastern religions—as for Plato[222]—it takes the form of reincarnation or metempsychosis, a continual passage of rebirth.[223] But even this process has to end somewhere; so for classical Hinduism it is *nirvana*, a blessed absorption into the Absolute, or for Zen Buddhism arrival at the Pure Land. This kind of pantheistic cosmic absorption into the Absolute Spirit of the universe is also familiar in the philosophical and poetic imagination of the Western world.[224] Ancient China and the primal religions of Africa and elsewhere took a different path. For them the dead (with certain qualifications) live on as ancestors. They become "the living dead" who may affect their living descendants for good or ill according to the manner of life they lead.[225] Another form of, as it were, bringing the deceased back to life is by ritual remembrance. Remembrance is a key theme in the Hebrew Scriptures.[226] The contemporary practice of memorializing the deceased, often in terms of sponsorship for charity (frequently for some exceptional action, usually physical, on the part of the bereaved) or keeping the deceased's social media accounts open, are modern variants of this. In such acts, in Holloway's words, "what we are doing when we use our imagination to remember the dead (it) is to bring them to life again if only for a moment: (it is) not *about* the person, it is the person herself".[227] A very different form of remembrance is the unusual experience of the bereaved "seeing" or "hearing" the deceased in the days following death.[228] But these are at best things which primarily benefit the living; they say nothing meaningful about the fate of the dead.

Curiously enough even professed atheism has not always managed to banish the concept of an afterlife. Holloway[229] remarks, from his long experience as a priest, that even those who reject any sort of life after death often fear death. Research by the Pontifical Gregorian University has shown that it is not unusual for self-professed atheists to hold beliefs about the afterlife and more especially about the reality of angels.[230] This seems to indicate that somehow the conviction that death is not the end of things is hard-wired into humans.

A number of people have testified to "near death experiences" (now called NDEs), often during surgery, in which they claim to have "died" and returned to life. Descriptions of such experiences frequently mention a sense of being "out of the body" and observing their bodies from above as though from a distance, and also of blinding lights, and even observing angels.[231] Though these are intense and very real experiences for the individual, it is difficult to generalize from them to give us a convincing insight on what it is to die. Doctors have explained them in terms of physiological conditions (especially during surgery) much in the same way as some neurologists account for visionary experiences.[232] They are problematic from a theological point of view in that such accounts seldom have any reference to the presence of God.

How then can it reasonably be asserted that we may have some knowledge of what might or might not happen after death? It all depends, of course, on what we mean by "knowledge". This is not a book on epistemology (the science of how we know what we know). However, perhaps some justification is needed that the contents of this chapter are not just groundless speculation. Philosophers who study epistemology point out that what is sometimes called "scientific empirical knowledge" (the knowledge that begins—and sometimes ends—with what may be discovered by our physical senses) is not the only kind of knowledge there is. We all, of course, have knowledge (including self-knowledge) of our life here and now, partly by the empirical knowledge of what our senses tell us, or how we feel (pain or compassion, for example). We also have *a priori* knowledge (knowledge reached by deduction or intuitive reflection rather than by sense experience). But we also have other kinds of knowledge.[233] Moral knowledge, for example, the knowledge that tells us how we should act, goes beyond the bodily senses. In fact, Kant, having demolished the traditional proofs for the existence of God, believed that our moral sense (his "categorical imperatives") provided the only real proof not only of the existence of God but also of immortality.[234] In addition, we have aesthetic knowledge, the sense that enables us to perceive beauty whether in art, music or literature, or in the natural world (the last frequently a source of wonder in the Psalms). So it is also possible for us to have religious knowledge. Audi calls this "experientialism", which, he argues, "grounds the justification of some very important religious beliefs in experience rather than in evidential beliefs or direct rational apprehension".[235] In addition to this it must also be recognized, as Michael Polanyi pointed out long ago, that there is no such thing as purely objective knowledge. All knowledge depends to some degree on the subjectivity of the perceiver, who interprets it according to his or her own assumptions and bias.[236]

So religious knowledge cannot be summarily dismissed. Of course, religious knowledge depends on certain assumptions (as does empirical knowledge), but this does not make it unreasonable or invalid. In trying to say something meaningful about "after death" I shall therefore examine critically the *testimony* (a crucial factor in all theories of knowledge) of the New Testament as the foundation document of the Christian faith, and suggest how it might be interpreted to relate to the twenty-first century. But it has to be acknowledged that both exegesis of the Bible and its application for today, especially in the field of eschatology (that is, "the last things"), are debatable, and others with different presuppositions may well come to different conclusions.

Life after death: a theological view

Aside from a very few, theologians too have shown a reticence to discuss death and personal eschatology (by which I mean dying and what might happen afterwards).[237] Perhaps this is a wholesome reaction to the overconfident literalism of much evangelical theology in the nineteenth century, which persists in many churches today. The problem is that to speak of a resurrection of a physical body long since disintegrated, an "intermediate state" between death and the final resurrection, purgatory and much else is not only fairy tales to the non-believer, it is also profoundly problematic to many (perhaps most) committed Christians themselves. As Macquarrie commented half a century ago: "The traditional eschatology of the Church has been of the deferred futuristic type . . . It still moves in the mythological ideas of original eschatology."[238] I don't think much has changed since then. But given that the age profile of most congregations more than reflects the ageing population, some kind of coherent approach to death and dying is as much an urgent pastoral necessity as a theological one.

It is quite possible to believe in God and not to believe in a personal life after death, as was the case in ancient Israel. The ancient Hebrews had only a vague concept of anything after death. Sheol, a shadowy repository for the dead, is probably not meant as theological dogma but rather a convenient concept (found among many people) that since the dead are (usually) buried they must be somewhere beneath the earth.[239] The greatest tragedy for the Psalmist, however, is not so much death itself as the fact that the dead can no longer give praise to God (Psalms 6:5; 30:9; 88:11–13; 115:17). The idea of immortality, insofar as it existed, migrated into two beliefs: the first that the ancestors, especially their deeds, lived on in the memory of the living for their challenge and encouragement;[240]

the second that it consisted not in personal survival but in the revival of the nation.[241]

It is generally recognized that the intertestamental period saw a great increase in speculation about eschatology in general.[242] Most important for personal eschatology (life after death) is the development of the idea of resurrection, probably in response to the conflicts of the Maccabean period. Resurrection becomes an event within the general eschatological development of ideas such as judgement, the Messianic banquet and last-times, millennium, the "book of life", and so on, and of course the Kingdom of God which is so central to Jesus' teaching. "Arising (or awakening) to life" (the term used in Hebrew) is first stated in Daniel 12:2, though it must have been a familiar idea by then.[243] [244]

Before looking at the evidence in the New Testament for life after death, perhaps a word of caution is necessary. Macquarrie—surely rightly—warns us that we must be restrained over claims about the afterlife. "Strictly speaking," he writes, "we cannot *know* the ultimate destinies of the world and of man . . . and this very lack of precision is an essential element in man's finitude." The New Testament too sometimes sounds a note of caution: "we are God's children now; it is not yet manifest what we shall be."[245] The basic problem, as we have noted, is that in the nature of the case we can have no empirical knowledge of something that is future, it is indeed "that undiscover'd country, from whose bourn no traveller returns". Christians might respond to this that we do have such knowledge of eschatology, both personal and universal (albeit limited), through the Bible and through the fact of the resurrection of Christ. I shall return to the latter below: but as regards scripture there is the serious hermeneutical problem of how we can interpret the eschatological language of the New Testament. There are, it seems to me, two issues here, though they are interconnected.

The first is the fact that the life of Jesus, and those of all the writers of the New Testament, was lived within a specific religious and cognitive context. They therefore had to employ the language and concepts of their time through which to convey the Christian message. C. H. Dodd helpfully calls this the background of the "mental furniture" of the Gospels,[246] and it includes the language and concepts of eschatology inherited as much (probably more) from the intertestamental period as from the Hebrew scriptures. The New Testament is in essence the original contextual theology. The issue for us is in deciding what is simply first-century transitory mental furniture, and what is essential to the message.[247]

The second issue is related. It is clear that the New Testament, like all religious writing, makes free use of symbols. I use this word in Tillich's sense of symbols opening up new levels of meaning and (unlike mere signs) participating in the reality to which they point.[248] Symbols thus have an experiential or emotional appeal which resonates with the believer. Here, too, there is a hermeneutical issue: how do we decide what is, and what isn't, a symbol, and what in any case it is meant to symbolize? On the other hand, there is a view that all theology is ultimately symbol or metaphor anyway, and thus cannot avoid using this kind of language; it seeks to express what is transcendent and is thus beyond literal empirical language.[249] On this view the hermeneutical problem will be that of finding new symbols which resonate with people in our own time and into which we can, as it were, translate the symbols of the New Testament.

There is also the more philosophical problem that we can only envisage the future through the epistemological lens of *time*. But if Augustine and others are right, time is a category which begins and ends with the present creation.[250] Eschatology—the idea of the "last things" or the end of the world—lies outside of the created world, and thus beyond accurate human knowledge or description; it lies outside of what we call time but we have to speak about it as though it is within time (this is in effect the impossibility of comprehending infinity whether in terms of space or time).[251]

So can we say anything more specific about personal survival after death?[252] It seems to me incontrovertible that many of the parables which are often taken to point to a future time of judgement (e.g. Matthew 25; Luke 16:19–31) are actually concerned to challenge behaviour here and now rather than give information about what might happen at the end of things. Comparatively little of Jesus' teaching is concerned with the end-time resurrection, though he clearly accepted it (Luke 14:14, "the resurrection of the righteous").[253] Whether or not Jesus taught that there would be a speedy coming of the Son of Man (Mark 9:1; Luke 9:26–7), he refused to give any timetable (Mark 13:32; Acts

1:7).[254] Jesus' reply to the question put by the Sadducees concerning the resurrection (Matthew 22:23–33; Mark 12:18–27; Luke 20:27–38) is his only substantive statement in the Synoptic Gospels about resurrection and looks at first glance like a trick question. The Sadducees denied the resurrection of the body and their question is something of a *reductio ad absurdum*. Jesus' answer seems to indicate that the deceased are in fact in some sense immortal ("like the angels", which the Sadducees did not believe in).[255] Jesus' reply refers to the Torah where the Lord says he is "the God of Abraham, the God of Isaac, and the God of Jacob" ("God of" is repeated for emphasis):[256] Since he is the God of the living not the dead, the patriarchs must still be living in some form. This does not strike the modern reader as very convincing, and it might just be that it is an ironic piece of rabbinic casuistry. However, it is more likely that it makes a serious point: relationship to God is such that it is not destroyed by physical death; death is a change to the individual's relationship to others and the world, but cannot change our relationship to God. This seems to be the point in Luke's account, which ends "God is not the God of the dead but of the living *for all live by Him*."[257] I shall return to this point below.

One of the traditional "proofs" of the resurrection of the body has been the resurrection of Jesus. Calvin, in refuting the opinion that the natural corruption of the body after death makes belief in a resurrection impossible, argues that the two reasons for rejecting this view are firstly, that the resurrection body will be in the likeness of Christ's resurrection and, secondly, that the power of God is almighty.[258] However, it is not at all clear how the resurrection body of Christ could be a model for the resurrection of the dead.[259] From a purely material point of view his body had not been corrupted by time and, further, some kind of continuance was necessary if after the resurrection he was to be recognized by his followers as really Jesus.[260] None of the words of Jesus after the resurrection relate to "final eschatology", they concern only the preaching of the gospel by his followers.[261] Calvin, like others after him, draws his evidence mainly from Paul. But it seems to me there is a problem here. Paul (as far as we know) never met the incarnate Jesus. The accounts in Acts of his dramatic conversion (9:3–6; 22:6–8; 26:13–16) indicate that there was only light and a voice (not a human form) and Paul did not know who or what it was.[262] Paul's own references to this experience (e.g. Galatians 1:15–16; Philippians 3:12—presumably he is referring to the same event) are somewhat muted. The "appearance" to him in 1 Corinthians 15:8 was clearly of a very different order from the appearances listed in verses 5–7 in that it was long after the ascension.[263] We cannot therefore draw any conclusions as to any "body" his vision might have perceived, and if Luke's account of Paul's conversion is correct, there was none. Paul's use of the word *soma* (body) is very varied. Sometimes it is literal (e.g. Romans 4:19, occasionally qualified as mortal, Romans 6:12 (see also 8:23), or as an agent of immorality, 1 Corinthians 6:13ff.); to be "out of the body" is to have an ecstatic experience (2 Corinthians 12:2–3). Elsewhere *soma* (body) seems to stand for the whole person (Romans 12:1). But he also speaks of the "Christ's body" in a metaphorical sense of the community of believers (Romans 12:5; 1 Corinthians 10:16–17). This should perhaps caution us that the meaning of *soma* is determined by the context in which it is used, and cannot simply be taken in its literal sense. In this light it is remarkable that in the key chapter on resurrection, 1 Corinthians 15, the word "body" does not appear until verse 35, when Paul addresses the objection, "With what kind of body do they [the resurrected] come?" His response suggests this is a rather silly question—"you fool!". His answer is to point out that God has created, and can create, all kinds of different bodies (verses 38–42). The imagery of the seed dying and developing into another "body"[264] illustrates the difference between the physical (*psychikon*) body and the spiritual (*pneumatikon*) resurrection body (verses 36–8, 42–4).[265] And as if to emphasize that the resurrection body will be very different he stresses the perishableness of the mortal body (verses 45–9), concluding "flesh and blood cannot inherit the kingdom of God" (verse 50).[266] Presumably this didn't satisfy all his Corinthian readers, for Paul returned to the issue in the second letter. In 2 Corinthians 5:1–5 he uses different imagery. Here the mortal body is an "earthly tent", and the resurrection body "a building from God, a house not made with hands, eternal in the heavens". I think all that we can conclude is that to speak of "body" in connection with resurrection is potentially misleading.[267]

In the modern context, then, we should probably understand "body" as a metaphor for the continuance of the self or person.[268] This was

Tillich's view. Arguing that Paul did not have a "materialistic" idea of the body, he asserts that "body" signifies the personality as a whole—"the affirmation of the eternal significance of the individual's personal uniqueness". He goes on to argue that the concept of an afterlife "assumes presuppositions about the nature of God, man, and their relationship".[269] We have discussed in chapter 2 how relationship (both to God and others) is fundamental to what it means to be human. On this view, an afterlife is not simply survival but a continuation of life in and with God. In other words, it depends not on what we are as mortal humans, but on what God is. Is there a biblical basis for this view of the afterlife?

The beginnings of the conviction that relationship with God is too strong to be destroyed by death are found sporadically in the Psalms. In Psalm 139:4–12, there is the thought that not even "making my bed in Sheol" can exclude God's presence, while Psalm 73:24–5 suggests that God in heaven will receive the psalmist to glory.[270] Psalms 16:10–11 and 17:15 probably refer to appearing in the Temple, perhaps after deliverance from premature death. What we have here is less a doctrine of an afterlife than the longing of deep piety for continuing communion with God.[271]

In some places Paul introduces the idea that "death and resurrection" is experienced in this present life: to "have died with Christ" and risen to a new life is symbolized by baptism (Romans 6:1–11). But this new life is still to be lived in the mortal body (verse 12: cf. 2 Corinthians 5:14–15 and 17; Colossians 2:12–13). He seems to argue that for the believer this spiritual death and resurrection transcends physical death and renders it harmless (Romans 8:38, 1 Corinthians 15:54–6),[272] and that therefore death cannot separate us from God in Christ. Elsewhere he visualizes entering into this fuller relationship with Christ immediately at physical death (Philippians 1:23).[273]

The language of the Fourth Gospel, despite its very different theological stance, sounds a similar note. For John eternal life is a present possession (3:36). Consequently the believer (in Bultmann's phrase) "has death behind him (having) passed from death to life" (5:24) and "will never see death" (8:51). The raising of Lazarus is an illustration of the truth that Jesus is the resurrection and the life, so "those who believe in me, even though they die, will live, and everyone who lives and believes in me will never die" (11:25–6). John's eucharistic discourse expounds this in the (for the Jew unthinkable) imagery (6:60–1) that "those who eat my flesh and drink my blood have eternal life" (6:54) which is equated to "abiding in me" (6:56). At the same time, the older imagery of resurrection at the last day is not entirely superseded (5:29; 11:24).[274] Clearly John is speaking of more than merely physical life (*psyche*). He uniformly uses the term *zoē* in this context, meaning "supernatural life belonging to God and Christ".[275] This characteristically Johannine idea can be traced back to the teaching of Jesus (Matthew 7:14; 18:8–9, 10, 16–17; 19:17; 25:46 and parallels—all of which use *zoē* rather than *psyche*).[276] Jesus' teaching again reflects the common Hebrew/Aramaic phrase for the messianic age, "the world to come".[277] We should then probably understand John's eternal life to mean a higher quality of life, unbounded by time and untouched by physical death, dependent only on the being and grace of God.[278] The Epistles to Timothy suggest that a similar concept was included in the liturgies of the early Church.[279] 1 Timothy 6:16 speaks of God alone as "having immortality" (*athanasia*, "deathlessness"), while 2 Timothy 1:10 sees the appearance of Christ as having abolished death (*katargesantos ton thanaton*) and "brought to light" both life (*zoē*) and incorruptibility (*aphtharsia*). While immortality, like eternity, is an attribute of God alone, death has been overcome by his action in Christ.

So can those of us who find eschatological literalism difficult, and try to penetrate the Bible's contextual conceptual furniture and symbolism, say anything very concrete about the afterlife (aside from the fact that it will probably surprise us)? Küng's view seems to me substantially justified. Rejecting what he calls "the naively physiological way as a revival of corpses", he argues that "resurrection means a completely other life, bursting out of the dimensions of space and time, in the invisible, incomprehensible divine sphere which is symbolically called 'heaven'".[280] And if that sounds too rhetorical, the Victorian priest and Professor of Classics Edwin Hatch put the same idea more simply:

> Breathe on me, breath of God;
> so shall I never die,
> but live with you the perfect life
> of your eternity.

I think that, for the believer, the only thing we can confidently assert about an afterlife is that physical death cannot destroy a relationship we have with God,[281] though what form that ultimately will take is well beyond our human comprehension. As the Spanish–Jewish poet Jehudah Halevi has it: "When far from You I die while yet in life: But if I cling to You I live, though I should die."[282]

So we live, forever bidding farewell[283]

Assisted Dying: a global issue

I have, in the preceding chapters, focussed on the case for assisted dying in the context of the situation in the UK. One of the main drivers of this situation has been that of an ageing population which is increasingly subject to multiple debilitating medical conditions. This problem is by no means limited to Britain or even to the Western world. It is a global one. In the late third century, Bishop Eucharius wrote of "this grey-haired world"; it has become a great deal greyer since then, as the reports of the United Nations Department of Economic and Social Affairs on world population ageing clearly show. The UN established its Population Division back in 1946, and it is now regarded as "a vital interface between global policies in the economic, social and environment spheres and social action".[284] It published an important report in 1956 which was mainly focussed on developed countries. In the 1990s, the focus was broadened and culminated in a wide-ranging report in 2007, which aimed at considering ageing populations globally in relation to social and economic development and human rights. Since then it has issued annual reports.

According to its 2019 report, "all societies in the world are in the midst of this longevity revolution", and now one in every eleven persons throughout the world is aged sixty-five or more. Projections are stark. It is predicted that by 2050 the number of persons over sixty-five worldwide will reach 1.5 billion (about the same as the present population of China). The populations most affected by this increase will be those in North Africa, Latin America, the Caribbean, and all regions of Asia. Additionally, life expectancy for all those over sixty-five will increase by an anticipated two years.[285] Projections suggest that by the end of this century there will be 155 countries containing over 60 per cent of the world's population—where one fifth of the population will be over sixty-five (in 2019 only seventeen countries were in that category). This, as the report points out, will inevitably put greatly increased stress on funding to support the elderly, and much of this care will fall upon their families. It seems more than likely that assisted dying, hitherto a concern of the Western developed world, will find itself on the global agenda. These figures should provide a stark warning that the ageing of the world's population is a challenge comparable to that of climate change, though it has received far less attention.[286]

At present, assisted dying or assisted suicide[287] has become legal in several countries, all (with the exception of Columbia)[288] in the Western world. The Netherlands introduced laws permitting euthanasia in 2001, which have been modified from time to time, Belgium in 2002, and Luxembourg in 2008. Both Belgium and the Netherlands allow the euthanasia of minors suffering from terminal illness, though it is carried out only in very exceptional cases. Both countries also permit death by lethal injection.[289] In America the state of Oregon permitted euthanasia in 1997, and it is now also available in California, Colorado, Hawaii, New Jersey, Washington State, Vermont, and the District of Columbia. It was also allowed in Canada in 2015–16. In November 2019, the Australian state of Victoria permitted assisted euthanasia,[290] as did Western Australia the following month. Prior to this it had for a period been carried out in the Northern Territories. New Zealand is, at the time of writing, preparing for a referendum to be held in 2020 which would allow euthanasia under strict guidelines. And it is also being reconsidered in Portugal. In February 2020, the German supreme court revoked as unconstitutional the law passed in 2015 which banned medical professionals from involvement in assisted suicide.[291] Regulations vary, and in many cases it is available only to residents and the terminally ill. Of course many more countries, including the UK, permit so-called passive euthanasia, "pulling the plug", in the case of the terminally ill. The country best known for its permission of euthanasia is Switzerland, and since it does not require the individual to be a resident it has been accessed by a growing number of people mainly from Germany, France, and the UK. Swiss law on suicide and euthanasia goes back to 1937, when certain restrictions on assisted euthanasia were enacted. This banned any active role by another person for whatever motive, and also criminalized "incitement or assistance to suicide from selfish motives". This somewhat vague restriction is presumably to be interpreted as meaning that no duress is to be put on the individual, and that any assister may not benefit from the death (hence Dignitas and other organizations offering assisted dying operate on a "not-for-profit" basis).[292] Referenda in some Swiss cantons show that there is no support from the general population for banning assisted dying, or for restricting access to it by non-nationals. It should also be pointed out that for residents of the UK who opt for assisted dying at Dignitas or elsewhere, there is financial cost as well as an emotional one. At around £12,000, inclusive of travel, accommodation and cremation, the cost is rather more than three times that of a funeral in the UK. For British nationals, assisted dying in Switzerland is an option only for those who are wealthy enough to afford it.

A changing landscape: medical, political, and theological perspectives

The Victorian poet A. H. Clough, in his ironic parody of the Ten Commandments, advised:

> Thou shalt not kill; but need'st not strive
> Officiously to keep alive.[293]

Clough was related by marriage to Florence Nightingale, whose ministry to the sick and wounded he greatly admired. His words reflect scepticism about Victorian medical practice. They have an equal, though quite different, relevance to our time in which (as argued in chapter 1) a philosophy of "keep them alive at all costs" has pervaded. But the tide appears to be turning, as the debate about assisted dying has become increasingly prominent and fast-moving. In the UK, opposition to assisted dying seems to be declining among medical professionals as it is within the general population. In 2019, the RCP conducted a poll of its members to which some 6,889 responded. While 43 per cent thought there was no need for a change in the current law against assisted dying (down marginally from 44 per cent in the 2014 poll), 32 per cent did support a change and the remaining 25 per cent declared themselves as neutral.[294] As a consequence, the RCP has now decided to adopt a neutral stance on the issue. Predictably this drew condemnation from pro-life lobby groups such as Care Not Killing, which prompted the President of the RCP to clarify that "neutral means that the RCP neither supports nor opposes a change in the law", and that it would now focus not on assisted dying but on continuing to support high-quality palliative care. However, this shift from opposition to a neutral position, he stressed, reflected the wide range of views among medical practitioners as within wider society.[295] Four years earlier the *British Journal of Nursing* had reported that a poll conducted by the Royal College of Nursing found that nearly half of its members supported assisted dying.[296] But perhaps even more significant are the views of palliative care specialists themselves. In 2018, Bobbie Farsides, Professor of Clinical and Biomedical Ethics at the University of Sussex, reminded readers of the *British Medical Journal* (*BMJ*) that she had been for two decades arguing that "it was logically consistent to be a good palliative care doctor" and to consider that for "some patients the best option was a managed death".[297] She is not alone in having been attacked for expressing such views. In April 2019, the month after the RCP announced its decision to be neutral over assisted dying, the *BMJ* ran a contribution from five palliative care consultants who opted to remain anonymous because they believed they risked their careers by speaking openly about assisted dying.[298] Their comments on the strong (and perhaps intemperate) backlash from some leaders and other members of the Association for Palliative Medicine to the RCP's statement regarding assisted dying are revealing and instructive. The five contributors particularly resented the charge that the RCP's neutral stance would lead to a breakdown in medical standards and to doctors being asked to "kill" their patients. They saw these charges as "indefensible and morally repugnant" interpretations of what was a quite reasonable attempt to facilitate a conversation, and as "blatant scaremongering". They stated:

> We, however, disagree that assisted dying is inherently a bad
> thing, and we believe that it is our professional responsibility to
> have an open discussion regarding the subject. It is important to
> do this since many of the dying people for whom we care have
> expressed a wish that assisted dying be an option that they could
> access.

They went on to deplore the fact that some leading members of their
association were taking steps to stifle (their term) discussion and suppress
alternative views. One can only hope that palliative care specialists—
whose views are of great importance on the issue of assisted dying—along
with the medical profession as a whole, will in the future be encouraged
to share their views openly and without prejudice. Consequent on the
RCP's statement of neutrality, the British Medical Association (which is
currently officially opposed to assisted dying) took the decision to survey
all of its 160,000 members in early 2020, and to assess the results at its
meeting in June of that year.

Opinion among GPs seems also to be becoming more tolerant of
assisted dying. A poll of 878 GPs in 2014 found that around 40 per cent
would wish to have the option of assisted dying if they were suffering
from terminal illness.[299] By the beginning of 2019, some 55 per cent (out
of 1,000 who responded) supported a neutral stance. On the question of
a change in the law the doctors were almost equally divided.[300] However,
43 per cent (up from 40 per cent in 2014) also declared that if they were
suffering from an incurable illness, they would wish to have the option
of assisted dying. The results of the latest poll conducted by the Royal
College of General Practitioners (RCGP) were released in February 2020.
Some 6,674 out of its almost 50,000 membership (slightly more than 13
per cent) responded, of whom 47 per cent favoured retaining the current
law on assisted suicide. However, 40 per cent declared their support for
liberalizing the law provided suitable safeguards were put in place. The
remainder were either neutral (11 per cent) or declined to answer. This
sample is still too small to be definitive, but it indicates how divided
GPs are on a dilemma in which they are at the forefront. The official
opposition of the RCGP to assisted dying, however, remains in place.[301]
Since more than half of respondents did not support this stance it would

have been more representative of GPs' views if a neutral position had been adopted.

The perceptible shift in medical opinion was emphasized during the most recent debate on assisted dying in the House of Commons. In April 2019, Nick Boles MP[302] moved a motion that the House should examine the functioning of the existing law relating to assisted dying.[303] The debate was called at the behest of the Secretary of State for Justice following statements by judges that any change in the law was a matter for Parliament, not the law courts. The Whaley case which had occurred shortly before (see chapter 5) was fresh in the memory. Boles explained that the debate was not to propose a new law but to try to understand, and provide evidence for, how the existing law affected those with terminal illness, their families, doctors, and carers. There were over twenty contributions to the debate, many of them recounting distressing narratives of the deaths of family members and friends. Some, including Boles himself and Liberal Democrat leader Vince Cable, declared that they had themselves changed their opinion and now were supportive of assisted dying. In response to the question, "What has changed?" Boles pointed to the shift in medical opinion (which we have discussed briefly above). He also highlighted what he termed the "consolidation" of public opinion. The most recent poll at the time had indicated that more than 80 per cent of the British public supported assisted dying for those who were terminally ill and had only six months or less to live. Significantly he also alluded to the resistance to change on the part of church leaders (with the notable exception of former Archbishop George Carey) in spite of the fact that the great majority of "their flocks" were supportive of assisted dying. The issue has continued on MPs' agenda. Six months later, at the beginning of 2020, the Scottish Liberal Democrat MP Christine Jardine introduced a debate in Westminster Hall. Similar concerns were reiterated, including references to the cases of the Whaleys and Mrs Eccleston.[304] Once again speakers called for further evidence of the way in which the law on assisted suicide was functioning. But perhaps by now more than enough evidence is available in the public domain. It has become clear (as Lord Falconer had forthrightly pointed out) that the Suicide Act of 1961 is failing those most deeply affected by it, and that the case for revisiting it has become overwhelming.

Boles was surely right to point to the institutional churches as being one of the most serious obstacles to reassessing this Act. It is this which makes assisted dying an urgent *theological* issue. I suggested at the beginning of this book that official church statements and those by many church leaders have often showed a surprising lack of theological depth, and have relied largely on secular reasoning. This contention has found unexpected support in a recent article by a political scientist, Prof. Steven Kettell.[305] In a wide-ranging analysis of ecclesiastical pronouncements, Kettell concludes that "while opposition to legalization (regarding assisted dying) has been underpinned by theological motivations, religious actors have largely adhered to the public reason criterion". While the validity of Kettell's classifications (theological, non-theological, qualified theological) may be questionable, his analysis clearly bears out his claim that spokespeople for the churches have significantly downplayed theological arguments, or at the very least have used them in a vague and ambiguous way, and have instead primarily relied on "public reason criteria". The concept of "public reason criterion" raises a number of methodological issues which are not under discussion here.[306] But it is necessary to note that it is a secular concept which disallows the validity of theological arguments, which it sees as ideological and partisan.[307] Such a stance ignores the fact that such a secular approach is just as much an ideological option as is a religious stance—every one of us comes to controversial problems with presuppositions of one sort or another. More important, perhaps, is the fact that historically religion, in all societies, is part of the complex which determines what "public reason" is. Nevertheless, Kettell's research is important in that it demonstrates fairly conclusively that theological argument has played very little role in the churches' opposition to assisted dying.

It is interesting that Archbishop Carey acknowledges that before he changed his mind on assisted dying, he too had adopted a kind of public reason approach. In his speech in the House of Lords in 2012, he had argued that there was nothing in the Bible or in Christian teaching which provided any help in addressing the question of assisted dying. Dogmas that human beings are created in the image of God, of the sacredness of human life, and indeed the sixth commandment, he thought were "too broad to be relevant". Two years later, and with the experience of witnessing the pain of those dying from terminal illness, he radically changed his mind—or perhaps changed his theology:

> For those who chide me that my change of heart is light on theological backing, let me tell you what theology is all about. It is about accompanying those very sick and dying people to the place where they feel abandoned, where they are already experiencing their own Calvary and Golgotha and where they need us with them to find their peace. If that is not theology of the best and purest kind, I don't know what is.[308]

His church, Carey concluded, lacked the compassion which is the essence of any theology that calls itself Christian, and was woefully out of touch with the people in its pews.

Carey was, of course, right to point out that there is no *direct* biblical or historical guidance available to theologians who seek to address the question of assisted dying—nor indeed could there be for it is a very modern dilemma. But, as I have argued in the earlier chapters of this book, the Bible does provide us with the theological foundations which enable us to do so: for it has much to say about what it is to be human with all its frailty, about human autonomy and compassion, and about life, death, and what might come after, and most of all about our relationship to God. To neglect this scriptural and theological underpinning and to limit the discussion on assisted dying to secular arguments is, for the Christian (as for the believer in any other faith), to leave out what is most fundamental to human existence. Of course, theologians cannot avoid engaging and grappling with secular arguments. But they must approach them from the sub-structure of their understanding of God and the world, and with the conviction that in matters of life and death theology has something important to contribute. It is from this perspective that I have tried in this book to explore the problem of assisted dying. If it has anything useful to say to the non-religious reader (if there should be any), it will be a bonus.

The Austrian poet Rilke's elegy (see note 283) beautifully reminds us that (whether we realize it at the time or not) each of us spends our life:

> . . . in the posture of one who is departing. As if he,
> on the last hill that shows to him all his valley
> again for the last time, turns, pauses, and lingers—
> so we live, forever bidding farewell.

In the ultimate sense, we are all in a terminal condition, for as the existentialists remind us, the only thing that is certain about our life is that it will end. The only question is when and how. We all, I suppose, hope that last farewell will be peaceful and not painful, as much for those we leave behind as for ourselves. But for those for whom the end days will be painful, compassion—both Christian and human—surely demands that an easeful death should not be denied them. As Desmond Tutu memorably put it in an interview as he approached his eighty-fifth year:

> I wish to help to give people dignity in dying. Just as I have argued
> firmly for compassion and fairness in life, I believe terminally ill
> people should be treated with the same compassion and fairness
> when it comes to their deaths. Dying people should have the right
> to choose how and when they leave Mother Earth. I believe that
> alongside the wonderful palliative care that exists, their choices
> should include a dignified assisted death.[309]

Select Bibliography

Ariès, P., *Western Attitudes toward Death from the Middle Ages to the Present* (Baltimore: Johns Hopkins University Press, 1974).

Badham, P., *Is there a Christian Case for Assisted Dying?* (London: SPCK, 2009).

Badham, P., "Assisted Dying: an international overview", *Modern Believing* 56:2 (2015), pp. 197–208.

Baillie, J., *And the Life Everlasting* (London: Oxford University Press, 1934).

Barth, K., *Church Dogmatics* vol. III/ii, tr. G. Bromiley (Edinburgh: T & T Clark, 1956).

Barth, K., *The Faith of the Church*, tr. G. Vahanian (London: Fontana, 1960).

Bartsch, H. (ed.), *Kerygma and Myth*, tr. E. Fuller (London: SPCK, 1964).

Biggar, N., *Aiming to Kill: The Ethics of Suicide and Euthanasia* (London: Darton, Longman and Todd, 2004).

Boyd, K., "Attitudes to death: some historical notes", *Journal of Medical Ethics* 3:3 (1977), pp. 124–8.

Buber, M., *I and Thou*, tr. R. Gregor Smith (Edinburgh: T & T Clark, 1958).

Bultmann, R., *The Theology of the New Testament*, tr. K. Grobel (London: SCM Press, 1952).

Buranzke, H., "Sanctity of life—a bio-ethical principle for a right to life?", *Ethical Theory and Moral Practice* 15:3 (2012), pp. 295–308.

Carey, G., "Reassessing Assisted Dying: a personal statement", *Modern Believing* 56:2 (2015), pp. 113–19.

Donne, J., *Biathanatos* (London, 1644).

Donne, J., *Complete Verse and Selected Prose*, ed. J. Hayward (London: Nonesuch, 1978).

Gawande, A., *Complications* (London: Profile Books, 2003).

Gawande, A., *Being Mortal: Illness, Medicine, and What Matters in the End* (London: Profile Books, 2015).

Harper, R., "Hans Küng's Theses on Dignified Dying", *Modern Believing* 56:2 (2015), pp. 121–34.

Heschel, A., *The Prophets* (New York: HarperCollins, 2001).

Holloway, R., *Waiting for the Last Bus* (Edinburgh: Canongate, 2018).

Hume, D., *Of Suicide*, hand-corrected text of 1755 downloaded from *open.edu*: emended version, published in *Essays on Suicide and the Immortality of the Soul* 1799.

Jeremias, J., *New Testament Theology* vol. 1, tr. J. Bowden (London: SCM, 1975).

Kitamori, K., *The Theology of the Pain of God*, tr. M. Bratscher (London: SCM Press, 1966).

Körtner, U., "Beihilfe zur Selbsttötung: eine Herausforderung für eine christliche Ethik", *Zeitschrift für Evangelische Ethik* 59 (2015), pp. 89–103.

Küng, H. and Jens, W. (eds), *A Dignified Dying*, tr. John Bowden (London: SCM Press, 1995).

Macquarrie, J., *Principles of Christian Theology* (London: SCM Press, 1977).

Mannix, K., *With the End in Mind: Death, Dying and Wisdom in an Age of Denial* (London: Collins, 2017).

Moltmann, J., *The Crucified God*, tr. R. Wilson and J. Bowden (London: SCM Press, 1974).

Moltmann, J., *The Way of Jesus Christ: Christology in Messianic Dimensions*, tr. M. Kohl (London: SCM Press, 1990).

Moltmann, J., *The Coming of God: Christian Eschatology*, tr. M. Kohl (London: SCM Press, 1996).

Rachels, J., "Active and Passive Euthanasia", *New England Journal of Medicine* 292:2 (1975), pp. 78–80.

Shakespeare, W., *William Shakespeare: The Complete Works*, ed. C. J. Sisson (London: Odhams, 1953).

Tillich, P., *Systematic Theology* vols 1–3 (London: SCM Press, 1951–63).

Tillich, P., *The Courage to Be* (London: Fontana, 1962).

Tolstoy, L., *The Death of Ivan Ilyich and other stories*, tr. R. Wilks, A Briggs and D. McDuff (London: Penguin, 2008).

Webster, J., "The Human Person", in *The Cambridge Guide to Postmodern Theology*, ed. K. Vanhoozer (Cambridge: Cambridge University Press, 2006), pp. 219–34.

Wiles, M., *The Remaking of Christian Doctrine* (London: SCM Press, 1974).

Williams, R., *On Christian Theology* (Oxford: Blackwell, 2007).

Williams, R., *Being Human: Bodies, Minds, and Persons* (London: SPCK, 2018).

Wyatt, J., *The Right to Die? Euthanasia, Assisted Suicide and End of Life Care* (Nottingham: InterVarsity Press, 2015).

Notes

1   See note 309.

2   Book of Common Prayer (1662), Burial Service.

3   *As You Like It* IIvii.

4   Mary Warnock and Elizabeth MacDonald use this phrase for their book *Easeful Death: Is There a Case for Assisted Dying?* (Oxford: Oxford University Press, 2008).

5   Figures from the Office for National Statistics (ONS); a Public Health England (PHE) survey in 2018 showed a further increase to 79.2 and 83.2 respectively. A more recent ONS survey though suggests that increased longevity has stalled since around 1980.

6   Richard Holloway, *Waiting for the Last Bus: Reflections on Life and Death* (Edinburgh: Canongate, 2018), pp. 2 and 19.

7   Atul Gawande, *Being Mortal: Illness, Medicine, and What Matters in the End* (London: Profile Books, 2015), pp. 6, 8–9.

8   So also Kathryn Mannix, *With the End in Mind: Death, Dying and Wisdom in an Age of Denial* (London: William Collins, 2017). Of course, these authors are addressing the situation in the richer nations. It seems to me that in much of Africa and Asia death in old age remains in the family environment.

9   "We spend our years like a sigh./The span of our life is seventy years/Or given the strength, eighty years;/But the best of them are trouble and sorrow", Psalm 90:9–10 (JPS).

10 I use the term "assisted dying" as it seems to me the least loaded; it is also referred to as "assisted suicide". The terminology will be discussed in the next chapter.

11 Hans Küng and Walter Jens (eds), *A Dignified Dying*, tr. John Bowden (London: SCM Press, 1995). Rosie Harper has an abbreviated translation of Küng's additional comments published in the second German edition of this book (*Menschenwürdig Sterben: Ein Plädoyer für Selbstverantwortung*

(Munich: Piper, 2009) in her article "Hans Küng's Thesis on Dignified Dying", *Modern Believing* 56:2 (2015), pp. 121–34.

12 Paul Badham, *Is there a Christian Case for Assisted Dying? Voluntary Euthanasia Reassessed* (London: SPCK, 2009).

13 George Carey, "Reassessing Assisted Dying: a personal statement", *Modern Believing* 56:2 (2015), pp. 113–19.

14 In his article in *The Guardian* (12 July 2014), "A dignified dying is our right—I am in favour of assisted dying." Tutu's remarks came in the aftermath of media exploitation of Nelson Mandela's last days and just before the debate in the House of Lords. Tutu declared, "I want the right to end my life through assisted dying". Two years later, on his eighty-fifth birthday, Archbishop Tutu elaborated his views further in *The Washington Post* (6 October 2016).

15 Nigel Biggar had already, in 2004, published his highly academic rejection of assisted suicide largely arguing from the traditional Catholic ethical tradition, with the somewhat contentious title *Aiming to Kill: The Ethics of Suicide and Euthanasia* (London: Darton, Longman and Todd, 2004). From a strongly conservative evangelical perspective, a former professor of neo-natal paediatrics, John Wyatt, published his informative but theologically problematic *The Right to Die: Euthanasia, Assisted Suicide, and End-of-Life Care* (Nottingham: InterVarsity Press, 2015).

16 The two books referred to in the previous note illustrate this last point. Biggar has only two references to Jesus throughout his book (both in quotations from other authors) and no other allusions to the Bible at all. More surprisingly Wyatt, writing from an evangelical position which usually lays great emphasis on the Bible, has only a handful of biblical citations, none of which are critically expanded upon. Jürgen Moltmann's complaint that Christian ethics has almost ceased to rest on Christian foundations seems justified in this case (*The Way of Jesus Christ: Christology in Messianic Dimensions*, tr. M. Kohl (London: SCM Press, 1990), p. 116).

17 John Gryparis, *Death*, trans. Aristeidis Pathanoglou:

> "He will be welcome, when the final hour comes,
> To close my eyes for ever,
> Whenever that might be, now or later,
> Provided he does not come like a wild storm."

[18] Surprisingly "death from old age" is not used on death certificates; apparently everyone dies of something specific.

[19] The implications of the resurrection of Christ for belief in the afterlife will be addressed in chapter 7.

[20] Epicurus wrote of "sleep, the brother of death".

[21] The clearest statement of "original sin" can be found in Article IX of the Articles of Religion in the Book of Common Prayer (1662). See further notes 22 and 23 below.

[22] Though "fall" (itself a metaphor) is nowhere used in the narrative.

[23] I use myth to mean the representation of an idea through a concrete historical narrative, a truth that can only be expressed in symbolic or picture language (rather like a parable). Exegesis of Genesis 2 and 3 is complex: Genesis 3:22 envisages a different tree from the "tree of the knowledge of good and evil" (Genesis 2:15–16), namely "the tree of life", the eating of which would bestow immortality. It is to prevent Adam from partaking of this tree that he is driven out of the Garden. One might see in this the all-too-human desire for an unattainable endless life. Adam (meaning "man") and Eve (connected with *chavvah*, life) are an individualization of the human race.

[24] Romans 5:12 is the *locus classicus* of the doctrine of original sin, that is that through his sin Adam infected all his descendants. This doctrine is not found before Augustine. It relies on the wrong Latin translation in verse 12, also found in the AV (but corrected in the RSV), "death passed on all in whom (i.e. in Adam) all men sinned". The Greek *eph'ho* (not *en ho*) cannot possibly justify this translation: it means "in that, because" (so RSV). This seems to me a classic example of a widely accepted (though morally questionable) dogma being based upon a false translation!

[25] More specifically, an *aggadic midrash*, which is not intended to expound the actual meaning of the text but is rather a reading of ideas *into* scripture (Louis Jacob's definition, *The Jewish Religion* [Oxford: Oxford University Press, 1995], p. 345).

[26] Moltmann has an extended discussion of whether death is a consequence of sin or a natural end of life (*The Coming of God: Christian Eschatology*, tr. M. Kohl [London: SCM Press, 1996], pp. 70–5). I recall a lecture by a retired bishop in which he stressed the grave dangers of the connection between death and sin, and narrating how, as the leader of a hospital chaplaincy group,

he had to exclude from hospital visiting well-meaning fundamentalists who
had this view and caused considerable distress to patients.

27 "From within the heart of man come evil thoughts, theft, murder, adultery,
wickedness, deceit, licentiousness, envy, slander, pride, foolishness." This is
in effect an exposition of the second table of the Decalogue. The traditional
Jewish view, that the impulses (*yetzer*) towards good and evil strive within
the human person, is reflected in Luke 6:45; Romans 7:7–25.

28 Partly through Martin Heidegger's concept of life as "Being towards Death".

29 John Macquarrie, *Principles of Christian Theology* (London: SCM Press, 1977),
p. 78.

30 Life is *psyche*, misleadingly rendered in the AV as "soul".

31 Paul Tillich, *Systematic Theology* vol. 1 (London: SCM Press, 1951), pp. 78ff.
and vol. 2, pp. 19ff., also *The Courage to Be* (London: Fontana, 1962), pp. 46ff.

32 As Abraham Heschel put it, "God is the meaning beyond absurdity".

33 Philippe Ariès, *Western Attitudes toward Death from the Middle Ages to the
Present* (Baltimore, MD: Johns Hopkins University Press, 1974).

34 A point made by Allan Kellehear, *A Social History of Dying* (Cambridge:
Cambridge University Press, 2007).

35 Wordsworth, who would have lived in Ariès' period of non-acceptance of
death, is remarkably prosaic about the fact and naturalness of death:

> But when the good and great depart
> What more is it than this:
> That man, who is from God sent forth
> Doth yet to God return?
> Such ebb and flow must ever be
> Then wherefore should we mourn?

(*Lines composed at Grasmere on the expected death of Mr Fox*, 1806); so also
the *Extempore effusion upon the death of James Hogg* (1835):

> As if but yesterday departed
> Thou too art gone before: but why
> O'er ripe fruit seasonably gathered
> Should frail survivors heave a sigh?

36   "Attitudes to death: some historical notes", *Journal of Medical Ethics* vol. 3:3
     (1977), pp. 124–8.
37   The high mortality from such causes, especially the Black Death, inspired the
     treatise *Ars Moriendi*, probably originally by a fifteenth-century Dominican,
     on the art of dying. It dealt with such issues as hope, temptation, Christ's
     love, prayer, and so on, and inspired a whole genre of such writing. Probably
     the best-known English treatise is Jeremy Taylor's *Holy Dying* (1651). For
     modern views of *Ars Moriendi*, see Kathryn Paul, "The *Ars Moriendi*: a
     practical approach to dying well", *Modern Believing* 56:2 (2015), pp. 209–22;
     also Carlo Leget, *Art of Living, Art of Dying: Spiritual Care for a Good Death*
     (London: Jessica Kingsley Publishers, 2017).
38   Gawande, *Being Mortal*, p. 156.
39   Gawande, *Being Mortal*, pp. 157–8.
40   Harry Sawyerr, *The Practice of Presence*, ed. J. Parratt (Grand Rapids:
     Eerdmans, 1996), pp. 62–3: so also Kwesi Dickson, *Theology in Africa*
     (London: Darton, Longman and Todd, 1984), pp. 185ff.
41   So called because the words were believed to have been written by the
     seventeenth-century Scottish theologian and Professor of Divinity Samuel
     Rutherford. In fact, the hymn is much later. Ann Cousin wrote it in 1854,
     basing the words on some of Rutherford's writings.
42   It was Urhan who premiered Berlioz's symphony for viola and orchestra
     Harold in Italy, after Paganini, who had commissioned the work, rejected it
     because it was not virtuosic enough for him.
43   He forbade its publication during his lifetime (he died in 1631), though he
     made careful arrangements for its preservation. It was subsequently published
     by his son in 1644. Donne would probably have known of Shakespeare's
     Hamlet, which was first published in 1603. But in contrast to the profound
     poetic and psychological depth in Shakespeare's treatment of suicide, Donne
     (though almost Shakespeare's equal as a poet) treats the subject with an
     almost complete lack of emotion and poetry.
44   Donne is writing before the word "suicide" came into use: his term is
     "self-homicide".
45   Donne uses an unusual form: the late classical form is *biaio-thanatos* or
     biothanatos, meaning "dying a violent death".
46   Donne had been imprisoned in 1601–2 for secretly marrying his employer's
     niece, but his subsequent life had not been so traumatic.

47   A theme he returned to in his sonnet "Death be not proud", which effectively mocks death as the slave of those who use their power to kill, and which itself will be "put to death" ("Death, thou shalt die").

48   Donne's interpretation though is questionable: while Matthew 27:50 has *apheken to pneuma*, the other synoptic Gospels have *exepneusen* "breathed his last" (Mark 15:37; Luke 23:46).

49   Whether or not the Jewish authorities in Judaea had the power to execute, this antagonism began in Galilee, where it was possible under Herod Antipas.

50   Joachim Jeremias, *New Testament Theology* vol. 1, tr. J. Bowden (London: SCM Press, 1975), pp. 276ff.

51   The highest causes of death were dementia (12.7 per cent, higher in women than in men) and ischaemic heart disease (10.9 per cent, higher in men than in women). All figures are from the ONS.

52   Or Shakespeare's "self-slaughter" ("Or that the Everlasting had not fix'd His canon 'gainst self-slaughter", *Hamlet* Iii).

53   First published in Paris in 1897, but not translated into English until 1957.

54   He thought that some cases of suicide could be caused by the society's failure to provide sufficient moral direction (anomic suicide) or conversely by its obsessive control (fatalistic suicide).

55   See e.g. B. R. Nanda, *Mahatma Gandhi* (London: Unwin, 1958), pp. 260, 262.

56   The mass suicide at Masada (*Wars of the Jews* Book 7 chapter 8) and the protest against Pilate's bringing the ensigns into Jerusalem, when the masses bared their throats to Pilate's soldiers (*The Antiquities* Book 8 chapter 3): he backed down and removed the ensigns. However, Josephus, perhaps in deference to his patrons in Rome, condemned these martyrs as "acting against God and themselves". Martyrdom, sacrificing one's life rather than denying the Jewish faith, came to be called "the sanctification of the Divine Name" (Jonathan Sacks, *To Heal a Fractured World* (London: Continuum, 2005), pp. 59–63.

57   He wrote to the church in Smyrna: "nearness to the sword is nearness to God, to be among the wild beasts is to be in God's arms." Badham rightly comments that "Christians did not see death as to be avoided at all costs, but one that might be legitimately accepted or even sought out for sufficient causes" (Badham, *Is there a Christian Case for Assisted Dying?*, p. 37).

58   See e.g. *The Acts and Monuments of these latter days, touching matters of the Church*, commonly known as *Foxe's Book of Martyrs*, first published in 1563 and later expanded.

59   Moses Maimonides, the twelfth-century physician and rabbi, and author of *A Guide of the Perplexed*, argued controversially that Jewish communities in Arab lands, when faced with the dilemma of conversion to Islam or death, should avoid martyrdom and convert since Islam was not an idolatrous religion. During the Holocaust there was a rethinking of the meaning of "the sanctification of the Divine Name", and it became interpreted by some to mean the obligation to *survive* in order to be a witness (*martyr*) to the atrocities committed by the Nazis.

60   Smoking was of course the rule rather than the exception through much of the twentieth century. George V died from lung cancer exacerbated, if not caused, by heavy smoking.

61   For the details see Sarah Bradford, *George VI* (London: Penguin, 2011).

62   Greek *eu thanatos*.

63   Wyatt, *Right to Die?*, p. 47.

64   James Rachels argues cogently that "active euthanasia" is not morally different from "passive euthanasia", since both follow from the same medical decision that "death is no greater evil than the patient's continued existence" ("Active and Passive Euthanasia", *New England Journal of Medicine* 292:2 (1975), pp. 78–80).

65   Tony Redding, *War in the Wilderness: The Chindits in Burma 1943–44* (Cheltenham: The History Press, 2015). The term "Chindit" was taken from *chinthe*, the mythical creatures whose statues guard Buddhist temples.

66   Wyatt, while complaining about what he calls the "euphemism of assisted dying" several times, uses the highly emotive term and misleading phrase "medical killing", which no doubt will be equally objectionable both to medics and their patients (*Right to Die?*, especially pp. 55–6). There is an obvious difference between *killing* someone else (where the onus for the act is on the killer) and *assisting* another person who has made a clear decision to end his or her life (where the onus is on the person who wishes to die). Wyatt reflects the anti-assisted dying position of the theologically conservative website Christian Action, Research and Education. There is a similar use of loaded terminology (but from a completely different theological stance) in the title of Nigel Biggar's *Aiming to Kill: The Ethics of Suicide and Euthanasia*, which

seems to me (despite his claim that he "takes a position in no man's land" on the debate) to be condemnation by definition.

[67] "What a piece of work is man, how noble in reason, how infinite in faculties, in form and moving, how express and admirable in action, like an angel in apprehension, how like a god—the beauty of the world, the paragon of animals; and yet to me, what is this quintessence of dust?" (Shakespeare, *Hamlet* IIii: the punctuation varies, the quotation is from the edition of C. J. Sisson, London: Odhams Press, 1953). Shakespeare seems to be echoing Old Testament passages: he would have been familiar with the Geneva Bible, which was popular in Elizabeth I's reign.

[68] Rowan Williams, *Being Human: Bodies, Minds and Persons* (London: SPCK, 2018), p. 47.

[69] The Hebrew Bible has several words indicating an individual human, but none for the abstract philosophical concept of human nature; the New Testament uses *anthrōpos* only of individuals, equivalent to *anēr*. Later theologians used *prosopon* for the abstract concept of "person", but the New Testament uses it in its primary sense of "face" (equivalent to the Hebrew *pnei*).

[70] The word translated here as "divine" ("*elohim*") is the word used for God or gods (always used in the plural); so some versions translate "a little less than God" or "a little less than a god" (RSV, NEB). In Psalm 89:1,6, it is probably used poetically of the divine beings of the heavenly court. The root meaning is probably "mighty". The LXX translates as "angels", and was followed by the writer of the Epistle to the Hebrews (2:7) in referring to Jesus.

[71] *'enosh* and *ben 'adam*.

[72] Macquarrie, *Principles of Christian Theology*, pp. 60–2.

[73] Neatly expressed by Wordsworth as, "Dust as we are the immortal spirit grows/Like harmony in music" (*Prelude* Book 1).

[74] Paul Tillich, *The Courage to Be* (London: Collins, 1932), p. 125. The nature of relation to others was explored in the highly influential *I and Thou* by the Jewish existentialist philosopher Martin Buber, tr. R. Gregor Smith (Edinburgh: T & T Clark, 1958). The idea of "human beings in community" is found in many cultures: cf. the common southern African proverb "a human being is only a person (human) in society".

[75] Williams, *Being Human*, pp. 28–48.

[76] John Webster, "The Human Person", in K. Vanhoozer (ed.), *Cambridge Guide to Postmodern Theology* (Cambridge: Cambridge University Press, 2006), p. 228.

[77] Macquarrie, *Principles of Christian Theology*, p. 37.

[78] Jeremias, *New Testament Theology* vol. 1, pp. 17ff.

[79] As well of course as "Mother", an image of God which is by no means lacking in the Old Testament: it usually uses the term "Father" of God's relationship to the nation rather than to the individual.

[80] Joachim Jeremias, *The Central Message of the New Testament* (London: SCM Press, 1965), chapter 1. Jeremias' contention that *abba* was not found in Judaism has been disputed: the rabbinic address is usually "Father in heaven".

[81] The New Testament term *metanoia* implies a change of mind or purpose, repentance: similarly the usual Hebrew term *shubh* has the sense of "turning around".

[82] *Nishmat hayyim*, literally "of lives", the word for life often is used in the plural for emphasis.

[83] *Bios* is only used in the New Testament of means of livelihood and therefore not relevant here.

[84] *Psyche* has an interesting history. In Homer it has the same basic sense of breath as the sign of life, and is often used of giving up breath in death. The *psyche* is also the seat of emotions and reasoning in human beings. In later Greek philosophy, it comes also to have the meaning of "soul" as the immortal part of human beings as opposed to the physical body. The New Testament very occasionally has it in this sense (Matthew 10:28, presumably under later influence). But the body–soul dichotomy is not a biblical concept, though it emerges in patristic writings.

[85] Biggar, *Aiming to Kill?*, especially pp. 18ff.. Biggar in fact ignores the Bible almost entirely: he has only two references to the New Testament in the entire book, both to Jesus and both in quotes from other authors.

[86] Heike Baranzke, "Sanctity-of-life—a Bioethical Principle for a Right to Life?", *Ethical Theory and Moral Practice* 15:3 (2012), pp. 295–308. Baranzke claims it first appears in public discourse in the Roe vs. Wade abortion case in America and was subsequently popularized by President Ronald Reagan's proclamation of National Sanctity of Life Day. It appears in some nineteenth-century Protestant theology and became particularly prominent in later Roman Catholic ethics.

87   The basic meaning of both *qdsh* and *hagios* is separate, set apart, i.e. devoted to the god and therefore sacred.

88   As Baranzke points out, the original meaning of the Jewish "sanctification of the Name" (*kiddush hashem*) was that God is honoured by *kiddush hachayim*, the sanctification of the life; that is, that it is by moral and ethical behaviour that God's name is glorified.

89   *Health Statistics and Information Systems: WHOQOL: Measuring Quality of Life,* <https://www.who.int/healthinfo/survey/whoqol-quality of life/en>.

90   *Shalom* has the basic meaning of whole, sound, safe. In Genesis 29:6 and 43:27, it has the meaning of "'alive and well, in good health", and in 2 Samuel 18:29 "still alive and well". In greetings the sense good health is implied.

91   Badham, *Is there a Christian Case for Assisted Dying?*, p. 65.

92   Williams, *Being Human*, p. 70; he developed this point further in *On Christian Theology* (Oxford: Blackwells, 2007), pp. 67–73.

93   This is the assumption of Judaism, that there are two impulses (*yetzer*) in humans for good or evil.

94   Tillich, *Systematic Theology* vol. 1, p. 84.

95   Franz Rosenzweig, *The Star of Redemption*, tr. William Hallo from the 2nd edition, 1930 (London: University of Notre Dame Press, 1970), p. 4. Rosenzweig though, as a practising Jew, believed that suicide as such was not the natural form of death and was counter to nature. But see also Jonathan Romain's discussion of rabbinic references in his article "A Jewish View of Assisted Dying", *Modern Believing* 56:2 (2015), pp. 103–12.

96   Wyatt, *Right to Die?*, p. 90.

97   Wyatt, *Right to Die?*, p. 97.

98   Keats, *Ode to a Nightingale*:

> For many a time
> I have been half in love with easeful Death,
> Call'd him soft names in many a mused rhyme,
> To take into the air my quiet breath:
> Now more than ever seems it rich to die,
> To cease upon the midnight with no pain.

99   Oliver Sacks, *On the Move: A Life* (London: Picador, 2015), pp. 377–8.

[100] Statistics suggest that chronic pain in one form or another affects around 20 per cent of the UK population.

[101] *Complications* (London: Profile, 2003), p. 121.

[102] Joanna Bourke, *The Story of Pain: From Prayer to Painkillers* (Oxford: Oxford University Press, 2014).

[103] See also <https://ghr.nlm.nih.gov.gene/SCN9A>.

[104] So e.g. the remarkable case of Jo Cameron, "the woman who doesn't feel pain" documented at <https://www.bbc.co.uk/news/uk-scotland-highlands-islands-47719718>.

[105] A problem exacerbated by the fact that difference between the dosage of opioids required to relieve pain and that which depresses respiration may be very narrow.

[106] There is a Visual Analogue scale 0–10 (where 0=no pain and 10=extreme pain), which doctors may use, but this still depends on the subjective judgement of the patient. The present legal situation, in which a doctor may prescribe drugs such as morphine to relieve pain, but may not do so to hasten death, is very problematic: apart from the fact that it involves reading the doctor's *intentions*, it places upon him or her the grave responsibility of assessing the dosage of a drug which can relieve pain without inducing death.

[107] In the New Testament *krazein*, to cry out (in pain), is an onomatopoeic term derived from the cry of the raven: the Hebrew term *hamah* (see below note 118) has the basic meaning of the inarticulate howling of animals, and is in consequence used of wailing in deep mourning.

[108] The terms *chil, chol* are literally the birth pangs, the pains of childbirth.

[109] Jeremiah 11:18–20; 12:1–6; 15:10–20; 17:14–18; 18:5–17; 20:7–18.

[110] The passages usually isolated as Servant Songs are Isaiah 42:1–4; 49:1–6; 50:4–9; 52:13–53:12. They describe the character and mission of the "Servant of JHWH". The question of the identity of the Servant, whether he is the nation as a whole, a remnant within it, or an individual, has produced its own library of literature.

[111] So Leviticus 13:45. There is parallelism in verse 4 where the Servant's pain (of sickness, *mak'ob*) heals our pains and his sufferings (birthpangs: *chyil*) bear ours.

[112] *nagua'*=beaten, stricken; *m'uneh*=humbled, mortified.

[113] Both in the Book of Deuteronomy itself and the Books of Kings, which argue that the nation prospers when it obeys God and suffers when it does not.

114 Matthew 4:23–4; 8:16; 10:1,8; 12:15; 14:14; 15:30 and parallels.

115 The "pains of death" in Psalms 55:4 and 116:3 imply the feeling of horror at the prospect of losing one's life rather than the physical pain of dying.

116 Recorded in Matthew 27:46 in the original Aramaic, presumably because it made such an impact on the bystanders. These are the opening words of Psalm 22, which contains a vivid poetic description of the psalmist's sufferings. It seems to me very unlikely this incident is an invention of the evangelist in view of the almost insuperable theological questions it raises.

117 It was not translated into English until 1965. I have discussed Kitamori in *The Other Jesus* (Frankfurt am Main: Peter Lang, 2012), pp. 63ff.

118 AV and RSV translate literally "my bowels (for the Hebrews the location of the emotions) are troubled": RSV, NEB and JPS have "my heart yearns". I think that Kitamori's "is pained" catches the implications of the Hebrew verb *hamah* more dramatically. He comments that Jeremiah 31:20 "literally agrees with the truth of the cross . . . no more appropriate words could be found to reveal the truth of the cross" (Kazoh Kitamori, *Theology of the Pain of God*, tr. M. Bratscher from 5th revised edition, 1958 [London: SCM Press, 1966], p. 59).

119 Rowan Williams (*Being Human*, pp. 75–6) maintains that theologians from the fourth century meant by the *apatheia* of God not apathy but "the possibility of intelligently shaping [a] response that is not purely 'self-protective'". Given the background of the Greek philosophical tradition (in e.g. Plato and Aristotle) to the anthropomorphology of Greek religion this seems to me difficult to sustain. If accepted it would not be dissimilar to Heschel's concept of *pathos*. Heschel has an extensive discussion of the rise of the doctrine of impassibility of God in *The Prophets* (New York: HarperCollins, 2001: original ed. 1962), pp. 318ff.

120 Kitamori, *Theology of the Pain of God*, pp. 23, 20.

121 Kitamori, *Theology of the Pain of God*, pp. 82, 147.

122 Kitamori, *Theology of the Pain of God*, p. 11.

123 Kitamori, *Theology of the Pain of God*, pp. 68, 147.

124 Heschel's *The Prophets* had its origins in his doctoral thesis at the University of Berlin in the 1930s. After the rise of Hitler, he took over Buber's position at the Jewish Education Centre briefly before being deported to Poland. In 1938, he escaped the Holocaust and settled in America. He became one of the leading rabbis who supported the Civil Rights Movement.

[125] Heschel, *Prophets*, pp. 291, 298, 348.

[126] Heschel, *Prophets*, p. 291, referring among other texts to Isaiah 42:14; 63:9, and Psalm 91:15.

[127] Most notably Jürgen Moltmann's *The Crucified God*, tr. R. Wilson and J. Bowden (London: SCM Press, 1974), but also Dietrich Bonhoeffer's *Letters and Papers from Prison* (London: Fontana, 1953).

[128] Heschel, *Prophets*, p. 624; also p. 620, where God is encountered as "a personal God to a personal man in a specific pathos that comes with a demand in a concrete situation". Heschel developed this theme in some of his other writings.

[129] William Temple, *Readings in St John's Gospel* (London: Macmillan, 1952), p. 385. Temple's book was first published shortly before the outbreak of World War II. He quotes from *Jesus of the Scars* by the World War I poet Edward Shillito, the final stanza of which reads:

> The other gods were strong, but Thou wast weak:
> They rode, but Thou didst stumble to a throne:
> But to our wounds only God's wounds can speak,
> And not a God has wounds but Thou alone.

[130] The idea that pain may be redemptive seems to me misleading: in Christian thought only the sufferings of Christ merit this.

[131] He was at the time Dean of St Paul's. The *Devotions* went through two editions in 1624 with a further two shortly afterwards. There was clearly an appetite for this kind of religious exploration of pain and dying.

[132] But see below on Tolstoy's *The Death of Ivan Ilyich*.

[133] John Donne, *Devotions upon Emergent Occasions I* (text quoted from John Donne, *Complete Poetry and Selected Prose*, ed. John Hayward [London: Nonesuch Press, 1978], orig. ed. 1929), p. 508. I have modernized the spelling.

[134] *Devotions*, p. 538.

[135] Shakespeare, *Measure for Measure* IIIi.

[136] Quotations are from Hume's hand-corrected proofs on the projected publication of 1755. A revised version was eventually printed in 1799 as *Essays on Suicide and the Immortality of the Soul*.

[137] Hume, *Of Suicide*, sections 15, 18.

[138] Küng, *A Dignified Dying*, p. 16.

139 But see further chapter 6 below.

140 Wyatt, *Right to Die?*, pp. 20, 70.

141 According to the ONS about a third of deaths occur in the home.

142 Kathryn Mannix, *With the End in Mind: Dying, Death and Wisdom in an Age of Denial* (London: Collins, 2017).

143 She has a moving example of this in the case of a young man on pp. 233ff.

144 Gawande, *Being Mortal*, pp. 111ff., 131ff. has several examples of this, some quite moving, others hilarious: this approach, he says, can transform the usual culture of nursing homes, which he characterizes as "boredom, loneliness, and helplessness"—the last thing the terminally ill need! The sentiment is movingly expressed in Tennyson's *Ulysses*: "Death closes all; but something ere the end,/Some work of noble note, may yet be done."

145 According to Gawande, 25 per cent of healthcare costs in America is consumed by the elderly in the last year of life and for very limited benefit.

146 Mannix, *With the End in Mind*, pp. 297–8.

147 Gawande, *Being Mortal*, pp. 149ff.

148 Also called narcotic analgesics, a group of drugs derived from opium and morphine, commonly prescribed since the beginning of the twentieth century in the form of codeine and its derivatives. Codeine is very frequently used to relieve moderate or mild pain. However, the BMA rates its overdose danger as high, and both in the UK and USA serious concern has been expressed about excessive prescription of codeine-based drugs and the likelihood of addiction. It is estimated that some 23 million codeine-based prescriptions were issued in the UK in 2008.

149 In America statistics for 2014 indicated that 3.8 out of every 100,000 deaths were from overdosing on morphine and related drugs, and that a further half million were struggling with opioid addiction.

150 Early in 2019 the Health Secretary revealed that between 2008 and 2018 more than 150 people in England and Wales had died from codeine-related illness: there were a further seventy in Scotland in 2016–17.

151 Gawande, *Being Mortal*, p. 155.

152 Badham, *Is there a Christian Case*, p. 92.

153 Guy Brown, *The Living End: The Future of Death, Ageing and Immortality* (London: Macmillan, 2007).

[154] Well encapsulated in James Thomson's *Verses occasioned by the death of Dr Aikman*: "Drag'd lingering on from partial death to death/Till, dying, all he can resign is breath."

[155] R. Munglani and A. Bhaskar, "Pain and suffering in cancer patients", *Modern Believing* 56:2 (2015), p. 159.

[156] Mannix, *With the End in Mind*, p. 291.

[157] Gawande, *Being Mortal*, pp. 125–7.

[158] <https://www.ndcn.ox.ac.uk/>.

[159] Wilfred Owen, *Insensibility*:

> By choice they made themselves immune
> To pity and whatever mourns in man
> Before the last sea and the hapless stars;
> Whatever mourns when many leave these shores;
> Whatever shares
> The eternal reciprocity of tears.

[160] It is interesting to compare Tolstoy's account of Ivan Ilyich's death with Thomas Mann's description of the death of Thomas in his novel *Buddenbrooks*. There is the same aloof family (apart again for a young son), the same physical and mental decline, but the moment of enlightenment is for Thomas followed by self-doubt and a return to prosaic German Protestant dogma. The shadow of Schopenhauer hovers over both deaths. There is a striking biblical example in the description of the decline of King David. While his sons were intriguing to inherit his throne, the old king's servants had to secure the services of a comely maiden from outside the capital to look after him (1 Kings 1:1–4).

[161] A key word in the Old Testament is God's *chesed*, meaning "ardour", usually in the positive sense of love, kindness towards his people (e.g. Exodus 33:19; Lamentations 3:22 and frequently in the Psalms 5:7; 36:6; 48:10 and as a refrain in Psalm 136).

[162] Also translated in the AV as "bowels".

[163] An alternative term, but which has no connection with the physical body, is "to have pity on someone" (*eleeo*), a word especially favoured by Matthew. It is usually employed in requests to Jesus for healing (Matthew 9:27; 15:22; 17:15; 20:30), but also of God's mercy (Mark 5:19; Philippians 2:27). The noun form came to have the meaning of "merciful giving". Similar in meaning,

but perhaps closer to our word compassion is *oiktirmon* (Luke 6:35). This word is used in conjunction with *splagchna* for emphasis in Colossians 3:12 and James 5:11; *oiktirmon* is used of God's compassion (Romans 12:1; 2 Corinthians 1:3). John has a powerful but unusual term in the story of the raising of Lazarus, where Jesus "groans within himself" (John 11:33, 38): the verb *brimaomai* means "to snort with indignation" but here implies deep inner distress. Surprisingly the literal meaning of compassion, suffer with (*sun pascho*), is used sparingly: Paul has it of "suffering alongside those who suffer" (1 Corinthians 12:26) and also in the mystical sense of suffering with Christ (Romans 8:17).

[164] "The *Thou* meets me. But I step into direct relation with it. Hence relation means being chosen and choosing, suffering and action in one . . . The relation to the *Thou* is direct. No system of ideas, no foreknowledge, and no fancy intervene between the *I* and *Thou*." Martin Buber, *I and Thou*, tr. R. Gregor Smith (Edinburgh: T & T Clark, 1958), pp. 24–5.

[165] Heschel, *Prophets*, pp. 398, 294.

[166] Donne, *Devotions* XVII.

[167] Though social media may considerably help in alleviating the problem of loneliness.

[168] Franz Werfel, *Lied der Gezeichneten*:

> Bevor du wirst dich stricken
> Zur letzten Nacht bereit
> Mußt du den Zwieback schmecken
> Der Ausgestoßenheit.

Werfel is perhaps better known as the author of the novel *The Song of Bernadette*, and the third husband of Alma Mahler.

[169] A moving example of this is the case of Marieke Vervoort. Diagnosed at the age of fourteen with a rare form of dystrophy of the muscles and spine, and also suffering from epilepsy, she went on to become a world champion Paralympic wheelchair athlete despite suffering extreme pain in the process. She signed a euthanasia request in 2005 in her native Belgium (where euthanasia is legal), but she continued to compete. Only in 2019 at the age of forty did she end her life by euthanasia. "I don't want to suffer anymore", she is reported as saying, "I am in too much pain. I'm done." Earlier she

had remarked, "I think there will be fewer suicides when every country has a law of euthanasia." <https://www.theguardian.com/sport/2019/oct/23/paralympic-gold-medalist-marieke-vervoort-ends-her-life-in-belgium>.

170   Tennyson, *Ulysses*.

171   Holloway, *Waiting for the Last Bus*, p. 72.

172   Holloway, *Waiting for the Last Bus*, pp. 83–4.

173   Wyatt, *Right to Die?*, p. 70.

174   Badham, *Is there a Christian Case*, p. 68.

175   *Hamlet* IIIi.

176   The lead author of the report, Prof. Sue Yeandle of the University of Sheffield, commented: "Caring is vital for us all and a precious support for those we love at critical times. Provided by millions of women, care also features strongly in the lives of men. Yet too often carers pay a heavy price for the support they give—financial strain, poorer health, social isolation". <https://www.bbc.co.uk/news/education-50465922>.

177   The Carers Trust calculates that there are 376,000 in the sixteen- to twenty-five-year-old bracket involved in caring for family members. A Department of Education report (The Lives of Young Carers in England, 2017) has investigated the impact on carers between the ages of five and seventeen, especially regarding how it affects their education and physical and mental health.

178   YouGov survey for Dignity in Dying, "What matters to Me: People living with terminal and advanced illness on end-of-life choices" <https://www.dignityindying.org.uk/?news%2F7-in10-pqople_%E2%80%93with-terminal-illness-support-law-change-on-assisted-dying>. As with most national polls the sample is too small to be definitive, but the fact that the respondents were all suffering from terminal illness suggests it reflects general perceptions.

179   Hume made the same point in 1755: "But suppose that it is no longer in my power to promote the interest of the public; suppose that I am a burden to it; suppose that my life hinders some person from being much more useful to the public. In such cases, my resignation of life must not only be innocent, but laudable." (*Of Suicide* Paragraph 15).

180   For Dignitas the procedure involves an oral anti-emetic drug and, after about half an hour, powdered pentobarbital dissolved in water for the patient himself

or herself to drink. In the USA similarly self-administered barbiturates are used.

181 E.g. by Wyatt.

182 The Greek has to abstain from wrongdoing (*adikia*), evil design, mischief (*phthoria*) and injury (*delesis*) towards those who are ill.

183 A survey conducted in 1997 by Ben Green indicated that nineteen out of the twenty-seven medical schools in the UK which responded deemed the Hippocratic Oath out of date for modern medicine, and used new variations of it along with GMC guidelines, <https://www.ncbi.nlm.nhi.gov/pmc/articles/PMC5747124>. The debate about the Hippocratic Oath therefore seems a red herring.

184 GMC updated June 2015, code GMC/WPSA/0718, also referring to the document *Treatment and care towards the end of life*. The code (6b) gives advice about lawful clinical options including palliative care and sedation "which would be available if a patient were to reach a settled decision to kill them self [sic]". It stresses that refusal of life-prolonging treatment is not suicide (Ref. 1).

185 Some advocates of the "slippery-slope" argument have drawn a parallel between assisted dying and liberalization of abortion, which, they contend, has led to an increase both in number of abortions and the justifications for it. I do not think that this is a valid comparison. Abortion may require an invasive physical procedure, whereas assisted dying usually involves only a self-administered oral drug. Furthermore, abortion requires a balanced medical opinion on two lives (mother and unborn child, the latter obviously unable to express an informed option): assisted dying is the decision of one mentally competent adult. I think that the legitimate debate over abortion, which concerns the beginnings of life, raises quite different ethical issues from ending life by assisted dying.

186 Biggar, *Aiming to Kill*, pp. 124ff.

187 J. Coggon, "Aiming to Kill: the ethics of suicide and euthanasia", *Journal of Medical Ethics* 32:9 (2006), p. 556.

188 Biggar's discussion is clouded by the fact that he does not limit the statistics to those terminally ill and that they include other categories of death such as suicides and neo-natal fatalities. Surprisingly Biggar accepts that "there are circumstances when it can be morally right to adopt a suicidal intention and

cooperate in suicide or commit euthanasia" (p. 146, also p. 162). It seems that here Biggar has one foot on his own slippery slope!

[189] "Better is death than a life of misery and eternal rest than continual sickness." Ecclesiasticus 30:17.

[190] Karl Mannheim, *Ideology and Utopia* (London: Routledge, 1960), p. 240.

[191] Carey, "Reassessing Assisted Dying", pp. 115–18.

[192] Biggar, *Aiming to Kill*, especially chapters 3, 4, and 5.

[193] Carey, "Reassessing Assisted Dying", p. 115. Canon Rosie Harper, in the same volume, puts it more sharply: "The key issue that those supporting some measure of assisted dying have to face from their opponents is that, whilst expressing due sympathy, they believe there is a super arching way of doing theology which trumps experience and causes the suffering of any individual to become the necessary collateral damage in order to uphold the principle." (Rosie Harper, "Hans Küng's Thesis on Dignified Dying", *Modern Believing* 56:2 (2015), p. 121).

[194] Küng, *Dignified Dying*, p. 25.

[195] Badham, *Is there a Christian Case?*, pp. 20–6.

[196] Küng, *Dignified Dying*, p. 25.

[197] Manslaughter carries a maximum sentence of life imprisonment but most cases result in a term of only between two and ten years.

[198] This, and the Purdy case, took place before responsibility for cases like this was moved to the UK Supreme Court.

[199] Diane Pretty died in a hospice two weeks after the case concluded.

[200] Her lawyer, Saimo Chahal, gives an informative account of the important aspects of the case in her "Human Rights: clarifying the law on assisted suicide", *Law Society Gazette*, 20 August 2009.

[201] Debbie Purdy died in 2014 aged fifty-one. She spent some time in a Marie Curie Hospice and at times refused food.

[202] For details see <https://www.bbc.co.uk/news/uk-england-stoke-staffordshire-49743727>.

[203] Reported in *The Guardian*: <https://www.theguardian.com/society/2019/apr/17/ex-supreme-court-jonathan-sumption-defends-break-assisted-dying-law>.

[204] <https://www.politicshome.com/news/article/ann-whaley-dignity-in-dying-respond-to-lord-sumptions-assisted-dying-comments>

[205] This law states that a person cannot benefit from another's death if they have "unlawfully aided, abetted, or procured" that death: this case is discussed in <http://www.ridleyhall.co.uk/assisted-dying-and-the-law-why-you-c-for -helping-a-loved-one-to-die/>.

[206] <https://www.dignityindying.org.uk/news/18-police-and-crime- commissioners-call-for-inquiry-into-current-law-on-assisted-dying/>.

[207] This case was considered along with a similar application from another man with locked-in syndrome, identified only as Martin.

[208] <https://www.telegraph.co.uk/news/uknews/law-and-order/9480227/ Tony-Nicklinson-breaks-down-as-High-Court-rejects-his-right-to-die-plea. html>.

[209] <http://thehitmix.co.uk/archives/2269088>.

[210] Not a slur on a great northern city, but because the advice for healthcare staff known by this name was first formulated by the Royal Liverpool Hospital in conjunction with the Marie Curie Palliative Care Institute.

[211] <https://www.nursingtimes.net/clinical-archive/end-of-life-and-palliative- care/what-is-the-liverpool-care-pathway-08–11–2012/>.

[212] They were revised again by NICE in October 2019 ("End of life care for adults: service delivery"). However, this advice does not give any concrete directions on what to do concerning hydration.

[213] So e.g. by Prof. Patrick Pullicino as reported in <https://www.telegraph.co.uk/ news/nhs/11779394/The-new-end-of-life-guidelines-are-lethal.html>.

[214] Details in <https://www.bbc.co.uk/news/health-40554462>.

[215] A third case, that of five-year-old Tafida Raqeeb, had a different outcome. She suffered a traumatic brain injury. Her parents wished her to be transferred to Italy, but the Royal London Hospital declared this was "not in her best interests". In this case, Barts NHS Foundation Trust's request that her life support should be discontinued was rejected by the court: for the comments on the judgement see <https://www.sciencemediacentre.org/ expert-reaction-to-the-tafida-raqeeb-case/>.

[216] <https://www.allaboutlaw.co.uk/commercial-awareness/commercial- insights/alfie-evans-the-legal-perspective->. The Children Act of 1989 gives parents the broad responsibility over what happens to a child, including the right to consent to medical treatment. I think most parents would agree that, after taking suitable advice and unless there are compelling reasons to the contrary, it is their right to decide what is in their children's best interests,

rather than that of the NHS or the courts. In July 2018, the Supreme Court
ruled that court action was no longer necessary in order to end life support.

217 <https://www.economist.com/open-future/2018/08/21/
the-law-on-assisted-dying-in-britain-is-incoherent-and-hypocritical>.

218 <https://www.theguardian.com/commentisfree/2014/jul/12/
desmond-tutu-in-favour-of-assisted-dying>.

219 <https://www.theguardian.com/society/2015/sep/11/
mps-begin-debate-assisted-dying-bill>.

220 John Donne, *Sonnet X*:

> Death be not proud, though some have called thee
> Mighty and dreadful, for, thou art not so,
> For those, whom thou think'st thou dost overthrow,
> Die not, poor death, nor yet canst thou kill me.
> From rest and sleep, which but thy pictures be,
> Much pleasure, then from thee, much more must flow,
> And soonest our best men with thee do go,
> Rest of their bones, and souls delivery.
> Thou art a slave to Fate. Chance, kings and desperate men,
> And dost with poison, war, and sickness dwell,
> And poppies, or charms can make us sleep as well,
> And better than thy stroke; why swell'st thou then?
> One short sleep past, we wake eternally
> And death shall be no more; death thou shalt die.

221 *Macbeth* Vv.

222 In *Phaedra*, probably deriving the theory from Pythagoras.

223 Beautifully explored in Wordsworth's *Ode on the Intimations of Immortality.*

224 E.g. Wordsworth's *Lucy* poems and Dylan Thomas' *And Death shall have no
Dominion.*

225 The deeply sacral status of the ancestors has influenced a good deal of
Christian theology in Africa (I have discussed this in *Reinventing Christianity:
African Theology Today* (Grand Rapids, MI: Eerdmans, 1995), pp. 94–8,
122–35.

226 *z-c-r* is especially used of the Exodus in the sense of "calling back to mind as
though you were there".

227 Holloway, *Waiting for the Last Bus*, p. 127. The Eucharist, following the tradition of the Haggadah, builds on this "remembering again to re-present the person" (*anamesis*). For Holloway "the only future life any of us can be certain of is the one we'll have in the memory of those we shall leave behind" (p. 136).

228 Oliver Sacks regards this as quite common and gives several examples in *Hallucinations* (London: Picador, 2012), pp. 231–6.

229 Holloway, *Waiting for the Last Bus*, p. 85.

230 Conference on Cultures of Unbelief, May 2019. The *theosthinktank* website reports that researchers at this conference claimed some 10 per cent of professed atheist respondents admitted to believing in some kind of supernatural phenomena, including life after death (*What do unbelievers believe?* dated 6 June 2019). An earlier survey for *theosthinktank* found that 15 per cent of respondents declaring themselves either atheist or non-religious believed in life after death, and that an astonishing 20 per cent believed in the supernatural powers of the ancestors (*Post-religious Britain: the faith of the faithless*). It would be interesting to know what proportion of these were of African and Asian heritage and from cultures in which ancestors are vastly more prominent than in the West.

231 There is a good example by Paul Robertson (the violinist and leader of the Medici Quartet) in his autobiographical *Soundscapes: a musician's journey through life and death* (London: Faber, 2016): see also Badham, *Is there a Christian Case*, pp. 78–80 and P. and L. Badham, *Immortality or Extinction* (London: SPCK, 1984), pp. 71–89.

232 This is not to say they are necessarily invalid as religious testimonies, for no doubt God can work through such abnormal experiences.

233 The eminent epistemologist Robert Audi has a helpful discussion of "Scientific, moral and religious knowledge" in his *Epistemology: A Contemporary Introduction to the Theory of Knowledge* (London & New York: Routledge, 1995), chapter 9.

234 He argues in his *Critique of Pure Reason* that "our moral sense, those obligations which have an unconditional claim upon us to act morally" are proof that God exists and that there is life after death.

235 Audi, *Epistemology*, p. 271. He goes on to claim experientialism "argues for the possibility of direct justification of certain religious beliefs without

assuming that there are any sources of justification beyond reason and normal experience".

[236] "The act of knowing includes an appraisal, and this personal coefficient, which shapes all textual knowledge, bridges in doing so the distinction between subjectivity and objectivity." Michael Polanyi, *Personal Knowledge* (London: Oxford University Press, 1958), p. 17.

[237] Among the few theologians who have written extensively on death are Paul Badham, Douglas Davies, and John Hick in his *Death and Eternal Life* (Louisville, KY: Westminster John Knox Press, 1994). Perhaps the shift in emphasis in the 1960s from existential theology to liberation theology contributed to lack of interest in personal eschatology. There are those theologians (like Holloway) who have ceased to believe in any meaningful afterlife, and others who perhaps regard it as well beyond the finite mind and thus too speculative to be dogmatic about.

[238] Macquarrie, *Principles of Christian Theology*, pp. 353–4: he continues that "this false kind of supernaturalism is not made any the less inconceivable by being quietly deferred to the never-never of the distant future". Wiles remarks that "to many the use of that phrase (the resurrection of the body) is a clear example of the archaizing tendency of the church to retain her old language and concepts, however inappropriate" ("The resurrection of the body", in *The Remaking of Christian Doctrine* (London: SCM Press, 1974), p. 126).

[239] The two words usually designating "living being" (*nephesh* and *ruach*) are never used of the dead: *nephesh* (like *psyche* in the New Testament) is often used of "giving up one's life". Hebrew has no word for "body" as such: *geviyah* usually means a corpse; *bashar* (flesh) may be used of man in his frailty. *Nephesh* sometimes (like *psyche*) is misleadingly translated as "soul", but it means the person, the individual living self.

[240] So the greatest misfortune was not to be lamented or remembered well—a fate specially noted of one king of Judah for whom, after an agonizing death from dysentery: "His people made no fire in his honour, like the fires made for his ancestors. He departed with no one's regret" (2 Chronicles 21:18–20).

[241] Ezekiel 37; Hosea 6:2 etc. Two passages in the Isaianic Apocalypse (chapters 24–7, usually taken to be a late insertion) are sometimes interpreted to imply personal resurrection but more probably refer to the revival of the nation (25:8 and 26:19). Job 19:25–7 is sometimes also claimed (*pace* Handel) to imply personal life after death: the text in verse 26 is corrupt but almost

certainly should be rendered "from (i.e. with, in) my flesh", meaning that he will see his vindication in this life (as the prose epilogue indicates).

242 The intertestamental period is roughly from 250 BCE to the Christian era: the Pseudepigrapha and the Dead Sea Scrolls of this period contain much speculation about the events of the end-time.

243 "Many of those who sleep in the dust of the earth shall awake, some to everlasting life, and some to shame and everlasting contempt." The English Bible can be misleading here. Hebrew has no exact equivalent word for "resurrect/resurrection": *y-q-tz* is used only in the future sense for "awakening from sleep" (so also Genesis 9:24 and 28:16). For the perfect tense *k-w-m* (arise, get up) is used. The LXX renders Dan 12:2 as *anastasis,* which is used often in the New Testament. The New Testament uses *egeiro* as an almost exact equivalent to *k-w-m* with the basic meaning of "arising, getting up" (Mark 5:41 translates the Aramaic *Talitha kumi* as *to korasion egeire*). There is an interesting example of the fluidity of the word (both in the passive) in the parallel of this narrative in Luke 7:14–15: verse 14 has "be raised" as addressed to the maiden, while verse 15 speaks of Jesus as "a great prophet who has been raised up among us". *Egeiro* (usually in the passive) is used of the resurrection of Jesus in the Gospels. The single use of the noun form (*egersis*) is in the curious note in Matthew 27:53. The verbal form of *anastasis* (*ana-histemi*) occurs only in connection with the Son of Man sayings (Matthew 17:9 and parallels) and with John the Baptist (Luke 9:8, 19).

244 Addressing God as the "One who revives the dead" is common in later Judaism, and was enshrined in Maimonides' *Thirteen Principles of Faith.* General resurrection is to take place after the restoration of Israel. The verb used is *chayah,* which derives from *chay* (life, usually used in the plural): it carries the meanings "to live (equivalent to *zaō* in the New Testament), to continue safe, to live again, to recover health". In this light it is questionable whether the Hebrews believed the dead were really dead in the sense of extinct!

245 1 John 3:2. The second half of this verse may be translated "when he is manifest" (the usual rendering), or "if it is manifest ..." I do not think there is any reference here to Christians sharing in the resurrection body of Christ.

246 The phrase comes from C. H. Dodd's *The Founder of Christianity* (London: Collins, 1954), p. 42.

[247]   This point is really only a variant of Rudolf Bultmann's thesis "New Testament and Mythology" in *Kerygma and Myth*, R. H. Fuller (London: SCM Press, 1964), pp. 1–44.

[248]   Tillich, *Systematic Theology* vol. 1, pp. 239ff.

[249]   So e.g. J. Schniewind's "A Reply to Bultmann" in *Kerygma and Myth* vol. 1, pp. 102–13. Personally I find this understanding of the task of theology quite convincing.

[250]   This concept goes at least back to Plato's *Timaeus* in which he argues that time began with creation.

[251]   Except maybe by mathematical symbols.

[252]   Theologians have debated the competing claims of futurist eschatology and "realized eschatology" (the idea that eschatology is realized in the present time by God's intervention into history and the experience of the individual). My own general preference is for the latter, mainly because there is clearly a timeless supra-historical aspect to the gospel as opposed to a futurist one.

[253]   So also in John 5:29 and 11:24–5; verse 24 shows that the final resurrection was a common belief, but there was no conception of an individual resurrection before the end-time. The idea that John the Baptist might be Elijah or one of the prophets risen from the dead (Mark 6:14–16) was presumably based on Malachi 4:5.

[254]   Interpretation of the Apocalyptic Discourse (Mark 13 and parallel passages in Matthew and Luke) is, of course, notoriously difficult, but most (all?) of it probably refers to the fall of Jerusalem, but perhaps also as a paradigm for periods of chaos and persecution (like the "Day of the Lord" in the prophetic books).

[255]   The comparison of the dead with angels occurs in the *Book of Enoch*, and a similar saying about angels not marrying or giving in marriage is in the *Talmud* attributed to a second-century rabbi.

[256]   The same phraseology occurs in 4 Maccabees 7:19 and 16:25 and may have been common in such disputations.

[257]   The force of the plain dative (*to auto*) is debatable: it might be (a) instrumental, by him (cf. Matthew 5:21, though in this sense we might expect a passive verb), or (b) in respect of him, with regard to him (cf. 2 Corinthians 10:4; 2 Peter 3:14), or (c) for him (cf. Mark 9:5), or (d) (unlikely) a Hebraism emphasizing degree. Barth's "participatory eschatology" (if I understand him correctly) seems to favour a kind of externalizing interpretation, that all continue to

exist in the mind of God (*Church Dogmatics* III/2, ET) (Edinburgh: T. & T. Clark, 1956).

[258] *Institutes of the Christian Religion* (1559) Book 3 xxv/8, tr. H. Beveridge (London: James Clarke, 1953): "The body which shall rise will be the same as at present in respect of substance, but the quality will be different; just as the body of Christ which was raised up was the same as that which had been offered in sacrifice, and yet excelled in other qualities, as if it had been altogether different." Moltmann, on the basis of Rom 8:11, thinks that "like the raising of Jesus from the dead through his life-giving Spirit, the resurrection of the dead is also expected as a physical happening touching the whole person" (*The Coming of God*, p. 69). Elsewhere he puts it more strongly and also includes the concept of flesh: "If there is no material 'resurrection of the body' there is no personal 'resurrection of the dead' either" (*The Way of Jesus Christ: Christology in Messianic Dimensions*, p. 260).

[259] See also M. Wiles, "The Resurrection of the Body", in *The Remaking of Christian Doctrine* (London: SCM Press, 1974), pp. 229–30.

[260] But, of course, we also have cases where he was apparently not immediately recognized, Luke 24:13–27; John 20:14–16.

[261] Though one might argue that the Farewell Discourse in John's Gospel is eschatological in intent.

[262] The closest documented similar conversion experience in modern times known to me is that of Sadhu Sundar Singh (I have discussed this in *The Other Jesus: Christology in Asian Perspective* (Frankfurt & Oxford: Peter Lang, 2012), pp. 38ff.

[263] The passive *ophthe* probably implies "appeared" rather than "seen by". Unlike the John of the Book of Revelation Paul does not engage in any description of a human figure.

[264] This may have been a common image, cf. John 12:24.

[265] Philippians 3:21 speaks of "transforming (*metaschematisei*) the body of our humiliation so as to be conformable (*symmorphon*) to the body of his glory": the first implies the outward fashion, the second the essential form. The genitive phrases (for adjectives) are Hebraisms. I don't think "body" here can be taken in the literal sense.

[266] Confusingly the earlier version of the Apostles' Creed (the so-called Old Roman Creed) has "resurrection of the flesh": The Book of Common Prayer replaced this with "body" both here and in the Athanasian Creed ("all men

[sic!] shall rise again with their bodies"). Calvin's catechism on the Apostles' Creed also has "resurrection of the flesh". Barth comments on this: "the notion of 'flesh' designates the whole man . . . The resurrection of the flesh is therefore identical neither with immortality of the soul nor with the body alone. It means the whole man." (Karl Barth, *The Faith of the Church*, tr. G. Vahanian (London: Fontana, 1960, pp. 136–7). This would make flesh, like body, a metonym for "person".

267 Wiles thought that body language in connection with the resurrection is not helpful, as it no longer expresses what it meant in the early church ("The Resurrection of the Body", p. 142).

268 Though "person" as an abstract construct in the sense used in later theology is not, I think, a biblical concept (*prosopon* is uniformly used in the New Testament in its original sense of "face", the equivalent of the Hebrew *pnei*).

269 Tillich, *Systematic Theology* vol. III, pp. 412–13, 416. But Tillich would also regard immortality as a symbol, since it is "not a continuation of temporal life after death, but it means a quality which transcends temporality" (p. 410): see below on "eternal life". Immortality in the Bible applies only to God, not to any "soul" of man.

270 Or possibly simply "honour" in this life (Hebrew *kabodh*).

271 Later Jewish thinkers interpreted Psalms 17 and 49 as speaking about life after death.

272 Here referring to Hosea 13:14 and Isaiah 25:8: the Hebrew and LXX wording differs, Paul seems to be paraphrasing. Both probably originally meant the restoration of the nation rather than the individual.

273 This seems at variance with a futurist eschatology, though we should not expect eschatology to be tidy and consistent. The idea of an intermediate state was an invention of the apostolic fathers, which later developed into purgatory.

274 It is not the case therefore that John has radically transposed the eschatological occurrence to the present, as Bultmann maintains (*Theology of the New Testament* vol. 2, tr. K. Grobel (London: SCM Press, 1955), p. 20, i.e. fully realized eschatology, but rather, in Dodd's words, it is "eschatology in the process of being realized".

275 Definition of Arndt and Gingrich, *A Greek–English Lexicon of the New Testament and Other Early Christian Literature* (Cambridge & Chicago, IL: Cambridge University Press, 1957).

276   *Psyche* is only used by John in the context of "laying down one's life in death".

277   *Ha 'olam ha ba':* to complicate matters *'olam* contains the ideas of "the world" as well as eternity.

278   *Aionios* (usually translated as "eternal, everlasting") originally meant a set period of time, but already in Plato it is used in the sense of that which has no beginning or end and is not subject to change or decay: that is, it is a new dimension and is qualitative rather than simply never-ending.

279   Both 1 Timothy 6:12–16 and 2 Tim 1:9–10 are fragments of early Christian hymns. See O. Cullmann, *Die ersten christlichen Glaubensbekenntnisse* (Zurich: Evangelischer Verlag, 1949), pp. 20–2.

280   Küng, *A Dignified Dying*, pp. 13–14.

281   Tillich argued that being accepted by God is more important than immortality: "He who participates in God participates in eternity. But in order to participate in him you must be accepted by him, and you must have accepted his acceptance of you" (*The Courage to Be*, p. 165). This is also the argument of John Baillie's classic *And the Life Everlasting*.

282   Jehudah Halevi, *Adon Negdekah Kol Ta'avath (Lord, Before You is All my Desire).*

283

> Who has turned us around, so that
> whatever we do we are in the posture
> of someone who is departing? As if he,
> on the last hill that shows to him all his valley
> again for the last time, turns, pauses, and lingers—
> so we live, forever bidding farewell

(*Wer hat uns umgedreht, dass wir/ was wir auch tun, in jeder Haltung sind/ von einem welcher fortgeht? Wie er auf/dem letzten Hügel, der ihm ganz sein Tal/ noch einmal zeigt, sich wendet, anhalt, weilt —/so leben wir und nehmen immer Abschied.* Rilke, *Duino Elegies, Eighth Elegy,* my translation)

284   UN Department of Economic and Social Affairs, Population Division: World Population Ageing, 2019, Highlights (ST/ESA/SERA/430), p. 2.

285   Surprisingly the one country where life expectancy is not increasing is the United States, but this is to a large extent due to self-inflicted causes such as obesity and the consumption of alcohol and harmful drugs (see <https://www.newsweek.com/deaths-despair-u-s-life-expectancy-falling-since-2014–1473848>).

286 Of course these are projections only, and there are many imponderable factors, such as deaths through armed conflict, epidemics, famine, and so on which cannot be foreseen (who could have predicted that 3 per cent of the world population would have been wiped out by these factors, along with the industrial murder of the Holocaust, in World War II?). Furthermore, as the UN report notes, population ageing does not necessarily imply economic decline as more over-sixty-five-year-old people may continue to be economically active.

287 The legal terminology varies so I use "voluntary euthanasia" here as equivalent to "assisted dying": the Swiss code speaks of "suicide".

288 Columbia has no law against assisted dying: in 1997, and again in 2015, it legislated to protect the medical profession in such cases.

289 Self-injection is allowed in Switzerland. There was a remarkable case in 2018 when the 104-year-old Australian botanist and academic David Goodall travelled to a Basel clinic, where he injected himself. Goodall was not terminally ill (though at that advanced age could not have had great life expectancy). He was frustrated at not being able any longer to pursue the discipline to which he had devoted his long life. A few years later he would have been able to end his life in his home country.

290 The debate in Australia is discussed by Stephen Duckett, "Arguing in the Public Square: Christian voices against assisted dying in Victoria", *Journal for the Academic Study of Religion* 3:2 (2017), pp. 165–87.

291 <https://www.bbc.co.uk/news/world-europe-51643306>. For a consideration of the legal position prior to 2015, see Albin Eser, "The possibilities and limits of help in dying, a lawyer's view", in Küng and Jens (eds), *A Dignified Dying*, pp. 74–93: in that same year Ulrich Körtner published his informative paper on theological approaches to assisted dying in Germany; see "Beihilfe zur Selbsttötung—eine Herausforderung für eine christliche Ethik", *Zeitschrift für Evangelische Ethik* 59 (2015), pp. 89–130.

292 Criminal code 1937 article 115. The penalty if found guilty of incitement or assistance is a sentence of not more than five years' imprisonment or a fine. A case in 2006, in which a person with a mental disorder requested assisted suicide, was rejected by the Swiss Supreme Court.

293 Arthur Clough, *The Latest Decalogue.*

294 <https://www.bmj.com/content/364/bmj.l1340>.

295 <https://www.bbc.co.uk/news/health-47641766>, 21 March 2019.

[296] 49 per cent were in favour, 40 per cent against: *British Journal of Nursing* 2015 Jun 25–Jul 8;24(12):629–32, doi:10.12968/bjon.2015.24.12.629: literature review article "Nurses' attitudes to assisted suicide: sociodemographic factors", by L. Evans.

[297] BMJ 2018:360 doi:https://doi.org/10.1136/bmj.K544 dated 7 Feb 2018.

[298] "We risk our careers if we discuss assisted dying, say UK palliative care consultants" BMJ/2019:365;1494 doi:10.1136/bmj.1494 dated 2 April 2019.

[299] <https://www.dignityindying.org.uk/news/new-poll-finds-majority-gps-like-choice-assisted-dying-available-discount/>, dated 17 June 2014.

[300] <https://www.gponline.com/gps-think-medical-organisations-drop-opposition-assisted-dying/article/1524830>: 33 per cent were against changing the law, 32 per cent in favour, and 34 per cent neutral.

[301] <https://www.rcgp.org.uk/policy/rcgp-policy-areas/assisted-dying.aspx>.

[302] Nick Boles was the chair of the All Parliamentary Group for Choice at the End of Life. He had earlier suffered a life-threatening cancer in his head, which had been treated by chemotherapy. Boles resigned from the Conservative Party during the Brexit controversy and did not contest the 2019 election.

[303] The wording is significant: it was "assisted dying", not, as in the Act, "assisting suicide". The debate was co-sponsored with the Liberal Democrat Norman Lamb MP, who is also a solicitor. The full text of the debate is found in Hansard vol. 662 for 4 July 2019.

[304] This followed discussions in the Isle of Man Parliament: <https://www.politicshome.com/news/uk/health-and-care/press-release/dignity-dying/109327/westminster-hall-debate-majority-speakers>.

[305] Steven Kettell, "How, when, and why do religious actors use public reason? The case of assisted dying in Britain", *Politics and Religion* 12 (2019), pp. 385–408.

[306] Basically it claims that the only moral and political rules that are adequate for common life are those which are justifiable and acceptable to the people as a whole.

[307] As Robert Audi puts it: "Whatever religious arguments one may have (in public policies), one should be willing to offer, and to be a certain extent motivated by, (must have) adequate secular arguments for the same conclusion." Robert Audi, "The place of religion in a free and democratic society", *San Diego Review* (1993), p. 677.

[308] "Reassessing assisted dying: a personal statement", pp. 114–19.

[309] Interview with *The Washington Post*, 6 October 2016.